Great Actors & Actresses of the American Stage

IN HISTORIC PHOTOGRAPHS

332 Portraits from 1850 to 1950

Edited by
STANLEY APPELBAUM

DOVER PUBLICATIONS, INC.
NEW YORK

For my godson,
Benjamin David Helfat,
who will admire the great actors of the future

ACKNOWLEDGMENTS

Thanks are due to two eminent historians of the performing arts for lending illustrations: Richard Koszarski (nos. 234 and 284) and Anthony Slide (nos. 270, 271, 272 and 312).

All the other photographs are from the collection of the editor and the archives of Dover Publications.

The editor's collection was acquired from many dealers in New York and elsewhere. He is grateful to all of them, and is sorry he cannot mention all their names. In the case of the present volume, however, it is incumbent on him to single out Mr. Ronald Alter of Ron's Now & Then, in New York City, who displayed exceptional acumen and assiduity in ferreting out a considerable number of hard-to-find images.

FRONTISPIECE: **OTIS SKINNER** (1857 or 1858–1942; father of Cornelia Otis Skinner, no. 210). Dean of the American stage at his death, he was revered as a tireless trouper associated with warm and picturesque roles. Debut, 1877, in Philadelphia. First played N.Y., 1879. Leading man for Lawrence Barrett in the early 1880s and a member of Augustin Daly's fine N.Y. stock company from 1884 to 1888, he also acted with Edwin Booth, Modjeska and Jefferson. A star from 1894, his great successes included: *The Honor of the Family* (1907; N.Y., 1908; also in 1926 revival); *Blood and Sand* (1921); and *A Hundred Years Old* (1929); but he is best remembered for *Kismet* (1911; filmed twice with Skinner; photo is from the 1930 sound film). In the 1931/2 season he toured with Maude Adams in *The Merchant of Venice*. Last appearance: the Players Club revival of *Uncle Tom's Cabin*, 1934.

Published in Canada by General Publishing Company, Ltd., 30 Lesmill Road, Don Mills, Toronto, Ontario.

Published in the United Kingdom by Constable and Company, Ltd., 10 Orange Street, London WC2H 7EG.

Great Actors and Actresses of the American Stage in Historic Photographs: 332 Portraits from 1850 to 1950 is a new work, first published by Dover Publications, Inc., in 1983.

Manufactured in the United States of America
Dover Publications, Inc., 31 East 2nd Street, Mineola, N.Y. 11501

Library of Congress Cataloging in Publication Data

Appelbaum, Stanley.
   Great actors and actresses of the American stage in historic photographs.

   Includes index.
   1. Actors—United States—Portraits. 2. Actors—United States—Biography—Pictorial works. I. Title.
PN2285.A7   1983   792'.028'0922   [B]   83-5184
ISBN 0-486-24555-1

Foreword

America has always been richly blessed with fine actors and actresses; this book is a small homage to the vast amount of pleasure they have afforded the public. It is a pictorial reference work, strictly photographic, ranging from 1850 to 1950. The basic arrangement is chronological, by generation groups; actors who had very long periods of service are placed at a point in time when their careers were most flourishing. The Alphabetical Index of Performers on pages 135 and 136 makes it possible to locate everyone instantly by name.

The stated cutoff date of 1950 means that no one is included who was not already prominent by that year. Thus, the book ends just before the most recent era, characterized by the full development of off-Broadway in New York (and its equivalents elsewhere) and the renaissance and spread of regional theater. Once an actor has been included, however, his career has been followed to the early 1980s: generally speaking, to early 1983 for New York stage appearances and for deaths; to mid-1981, for stage appearances outside of New York.

Only actors who performed in English are represented. A mere handful of British visitors are included (as opposed to the numerous British and other foreign actors, legitimately included, who became an integral part of the American scene). Actors essentially associated with musicals have already been covered in the companion volume to this one, *Stars of the American Musical Theater in Historic Photographs, 1860s to 1950* (by Appelbaum and Camner; Dover 0-486-24209-9); only a very few of these are also included in the present volume, because of the unusually versatile nature of their career. Actors who appeared in plays, but whose film work overwhelms their stage work in significance, are also omitted; in this area, the choice was necessarily very subjective but, it is hoped, not capricious. Even with all these limitations, the huge number of candidates for inclusion still made a rigorous selection inevitable, especially in the nineteenth century, which is represented by only a small sampling of exceedingly great and/or popular figures; but—for the period 1900–1950, at least—just about every real star, and a generous number of interesting character actors, will be found here.

Since the book is chiefly a visual reference tool, the captions had to be very brief; they cannot be considered as adequate biographies, but merely as capsule summaries of the performers'

professional (chiefly stage) work. Nevertheless, the information contained in the captions has been culled from a multitude of biographical dictionaries, full-length biographies, memoirs, yearbooks, chronicles, reviews, obituaries, original programs and similar sources. Birth years given here may be earlier than those supplied to the press by performers in mid-career; in such cases, older reference books or posthumous accounts were the sources for the earlier dates; no doubt, even some of those printed here will eventually have to be moved backward. All actors were born in the United States unless otherwise stated. Marriages and other relationships are usually given only when the spouse or relative was also in the theater, especially when he or she is also included in the book.

Emphasis has been placed on the actor's length of service before the public; that is, an effort has been made to ascertain the earliest and latest dates of acting on the stage. It will be noted in the captions that this book is truly concerned with the *American* theater, not just that of New York City; it is fascinating to see, for instance, what an important nursery of acting talent San Francisco was in the second half of the nineteenth century and the beginning of the twentieth. Nevertheless, since New York was the nation's theatrical Mecca in the period covered, and especially since its stage is the one that has been most thoroughly chronicled, it was impossible not to use New York as a constant point of reference (all cited performances are there unless otherwise stated).

Plays cited are those of lasting value or of great importance in a performer's career. They are always New York premieres unless specifically identified as revivals (no such identification for Shakespeare and the like).

The section "Notes on the Photographs" on pages 133 and 134 supplies the names of all identified photographers, dates the pictures wherever possible, and includes certain other information about the pictures that would have cluttered the captions. Many outstanding portrait photographers are represented here, although for the purposes of this volume—clear identification of the subject's features—it was often necessary to disregard the original framing and composition and to crop in more closely to the face.

1. JUNIUS BRUTUS BOOTH, SR. (1796–1852; born in England; father of John Wilkes Booth, no. 11, and of Edwin Booth, no. 19, who is also seen in the present photo). The first top-level English actor to make his home in this country, acting from coast to coast. Debut, 1813, in England; 1817, London, where he was recklessly pitted against the idolized Edmund Kean. To the U.S., 1821 (played first in Virginia; then in N.Y., same year). Famed for his Shakespeare and other heavy tragedy, notorious for his drinking and wild eccentricities. European trips, 1825–27 and 1836. From 1849, accompanied on his tours by Edwin, who stayed behind in California in 1852 while Junius traveled to New Orleans and died on a Mississippi steamboat. **2. CHARLOTTE** Saunders **CUSHMAN** (1816–1876). Greatest 19th-century American actress. Began as a singer: concerts (from 1830) and opera (1835) in her native Boston. In New Orleans, 1836, lost her singing voice and turned to the speaking stage; N.Y. debut, same year, as Lady Macbeth. First played Romeo, 1837, N.Y.; remained fond of masculine roles. Although chiefly admired in Shakespeare and as the gypsy hag Meg Merrilies, she was also the first American Lady Gay Spanker in *London Assurance* (1841). At Macready's request, she acted with him in his 1843/4 American season, then accompanied him to England (1844–48), enjoying tremendous success there. After several tentative retirements, she made her real farewell to N.Y. in 1874, subsequently taking leave of Philadelphia, 1874, and Boston, 1875.

3

4

Two mighty rivals, protagonists of the Astor Place riot. **3. WILLIAM CHARLES MACREADY** (English; 1793–1873). Foremost English actor of his generation, innovator in production (greater historical accuracy) as well as performance (more restraint, greater feeling for ensemble). Son of a provincial manager, he made his debut in Birmingham, 1810; London debut, 1816. Outstanding in Shakespeare, he also created major roles written for him by Knowles and Bulwer. First U.S. tour, 1826/7; second 1843/4; the third, 1848/9, culminated in the Astor Place (N.Y.) riot of May 10, 1849, fomented by jingoistic "know-nothing" adherents of his American nemesis Forrest (22 rioters killed and 36 wounded by militia artillery). Retirement, 1851. **4. EDWIN FORREST** (1806–1872). A major American tragedian. Though far from an insensitive ranter, he exploited his physical strength in his acting—unlike the cold and suave Macready, who was a direct rival as early as 1826 (Forrest's first N.Y. appearance; his debut

had been in Philadelphia in 1820 and he had toured extensively in the interim). In the 1830s Forrest appeared in England and Europe (1834–37) and created in N.Y. roles that Macready had originally done in London (as in *The Lady of Lyons*, 1838, and *Richelieu*, 1839, both written by Bulwer). The next decade saw more outspoken rivalry (Macready in the U.S., 1843; Forrest in England, 1845), culminating in the bloody riot of 1849. Forrest, active all his life (farewell to N.Y., 1871; a last reading in Brooklyn, 1872), endowed the Edwin Forrest home for retired actors in his will. Perhaps his greatest benefit to the American stage was his encouragement of native playwrights. *Metamora* (first performance, N.Y., 1829), *The Gladiator* (N.Y., 1831), *The Broker of Bogota* (N.Y., 1834) and *Jack Cade* (N.Y., 1841) were among the plays written expressly for him (his role in these works was often that of an oppressed fighter for freedom).

6

5. F(rancis) **S. CHANFRAU** (1824–1884). Beginning as a super at the Bowery Theatre in 1840, he became a dependable all-around actor and manager in N.Y. In 1848, in the comic play *A Glance at New York* (subsequently imitated all over the country), he created the role of Mose, a colorful young volunteer fireman from the lowest social ranks of the city; he continued to enact Mose in numerous sequels. The main role of his later years (first N.Y. performance, 1871) was in *Kit, the Arkansas Traveller.* **6. EDGAR LOOMIS DAVENPORT** (1815–1877; father of Fanny Davenport, no. 52). Debut, 1836, in Providence; N.Y., 1843. After floundering in comedy and melodrama, he became the leading man of the playwright/actress Anna Cora Mowatt (1846–50), accompanying her to England in 1847. Back in the U.S. in 1854, he enjoyed a varied and rich career without ever reaching the pinnacle of success that many felt he deserved. Highlights: creation of the role of Lanciotto in Boker's *Francesca da Rimini* (N.Y., 1855); acting partnership with James W. Wallack, Jr. (cousin of Lester Wallack, no. 29), between 1861 and 1868. Last N.Y. appearance (in support of Lawrence Barrett), 1876; played Philadelphia, 1877. Several of his children had important acting careers. **7. JAMES H**(enry) **HACKETT** (1800–1871; father of James K. Hackett, no. 57). A merchant who married an actress and then went on the stage himself (N.Y., 1826), he was one of the first and best Yankee comedians (New England rural types) and a great fosterer of native playwriting. Many trips to England, where he was much admired as Falstaff (first undertaken in N.Y., 1833). Other important plays: *The Times, or Life in New York* (1829); a pre-Jefferson *Rip Van Winkle* (1830); *The Lion of the West* (1831); and *The Kentuckian* (1833). His last regular appearance in the N.Y. area was in Brooklyn, 1870. Also an important theatrical manager and director of opera (he brought Mario and Grisi to the U.S. in 1854, and in that year they were the very first attraction at the N.Y. Academy of Music).

8

9

8. MRS. JOHN DREW (Louisa Lane [Crane] Drew, 1818–1897; born in England; mother of the younger John Drew, no. 69; grandmother of the Barrymores, nos. 74–76). Daughter of an actor, she was on stage from infancy. She came to the U.S. in 1827 (debut in Philadelphia); N.Y. debut, 1828. Very active all over the U.S. and the Caribbean, with Philadelphia as her base. In 1853, in that city, she and John Drew, her third husband (married 1850), went into a partnership with William Wheatly at the Arch Street Theatre. By 1861 she was running the Arch Street alone (Drew died in 1862), and she continued to do so until 1892. Her acting career ended only with her death. Most famous in her last years as Mrs. Malaprop in all-star touring revivals of *The Rivals* (1882 ff., 1896). **9. LAURA KEENE** (ca. 1820–1873; born in England; real name Mary Moss). After acting in London with Madame Vestris (from whom she probably imbibed the constant urge to manage her own theaters), she made her U.S. debut at Wallack's Theatre, N.Y., 1852. After ventures in Baltimore, California and Australia, she returned to N.Y. in 1855, taking over the Varieties Theatre there and then (1856–63) running the new Laura Keene's Theatre, where she produced and acted in such plays as: *The Marble Heart* (1856); *Our American Cousin* (1858; longest run in the U.S. up to that time); *Jeanie Deans* and *The Colleen Bawn* (both by Boucicault, both 1860); and *The Seven Sisters* (1861). After 1863 she was chiefly a traveling star. In 1865 she was present at Lincoln's assassination (at a Ford's Theatre revival of *Our American Cousin*). Her last managerial attempt (N.Y., 1871) was a failure; her last acting appearance in N.Y. was in 1872. **10. JOSEPH JEFFERSON** (III; 1829–1905). Representing the fourth generation of a great clan of actors, he was on stage at age 3. After a N.Y. appearance in 1837, he spent 12 years roaming the nation with his family. Great success back in N.Y., 1849. In 1857/8, lead comedian for Laura Keene (including *Our American Cousin*, 1858). In 1859/60, at (N.Y.) Winter Garden under Boucicault in *The Cricket on the Hearth* and *The Octoroon* (both 1859) and a tentative version of *Rip Van Winkle* (1860). From 1861 to 1865, in California and Australia. In the revised *Rip Van Winkle*, London, 1865; N.Y., 1866. From 1870 until his last performance (Paterson, 1904) played only five different roles, especially the much-loved Rip.

11

12

11. JOHN WILKES BOOTH (1838–1865; son of Junius Brutus Booth, Sr., no. 1; brother of Edwin Booth, no. 19). Youngest of three acting brothers (the eldest being Junius Brutus Booth, Jr.), he made his debut in Baltimore in 1855. In 1857 he played for the Drews at the Arch Street in Philadelphia. N.Y. debut, 1862, as Richard III; most important appearance there, November 25, 1864, as Mark Antony in *Julius Caesar* with his brothers as Brutus and Cassius. A romantic but unstable actor, he may have drifted into political agitation out of despair over losing his voice. Killed by pursuers after his assassination of Lincoln.   **12. ADAH ISAACS MENKEN** (1835–1868; maiden name uncertain; "Isaacs Menken" was derived from the first of her several husbands). Danseuse, actress, poet, she is probably most important as a legend. Acting debut, 1857, in her native Louisiana; N.Y. debut, 1859. In Albany, 1861, she first enacted the masculine title role of *Mazeppa* (earlier done by men; her costuming left no doubt as to her sex); her first N.Y. *Mazeppa*, 1862. Triumphal appearances in San Francisco, 1863/4; first trip to England, 1864. Last N.Y. performances, 1866, then back to England (and France). Liaisons with Swinburne and Dumas *père*.

13

14

15

13. AGNES Kelly **ROBERTSON** (Scottish; 1833–1916). First sang in public at age 11, acted at 13. Protégée of Charles Kean, London, 1851–53. To U.S., 1853, with husband (?) Boucicault; great success there in his plays, especially *Jessie Brown* (1858), *The Octoroon* (1859) and *The Colleen Bawn* (1860). Back to London with him, 1860. Later N.Y. appearances: 1872, 1879, 1881, 1890 (a benefit for her; she had been repudiated by Boucicault in 1888). Some London appearances in the 1890s. **14. DION BOUCICAULT**, Sr. (Dionysius Lardner Bourcicault; Irish; 1820 or 1822–1890). One of the most industrious and picturesque 19th-century actors and playwrights, specializing from 1860 on in Irish folk plays that influenced Synge and Shaw; some were revived at the Abbey, Dublin, in the 1970s. Debut, 1838, in England as "Lee Moreton"; fame for play *London Assurance*, 1841. London acting debut, 1852. To U.S. with Agnes Robertson, 1853, but he did not act there until the next year. Associated with Laura Keene in N.Y. later in the 1850s. Back in London, 1860–66 and for periods thereafter (later great plays: *Arrah na Pogue*, 1865; *The Shaughraun*, 1874). Acted (also taught and lectured) in N.Y. to about 1889; still writing and directing there, 1890. Pioneer in the fight for playwrights' royalties and in the institution of multiple road companies of N.Y. hits. **15. WILLIAM WARREN** (Jr., 1812–1888; cousin of Joseph Jefferson, no. 10). Son and namesake of important actor/manager of the Chestnut Street Theatre in Philadelphia, he made his debut in that city in 1832; N.Y. debut, 1841; English visit, 1845. From 1847 until his retirement in 1883 (except for a single starring tour, 1864/5) he was at the Boston Museum, where he gained affection and acclaim as the greatest stock actor in the country, excelling in hundreds of roles.

16. CHARLES Albert **FECHTER** (1824–1879; French/English, born in London). Began acting in Paris, ca. 1840; with the Comédie-Française, 1844–46. Created the role of Armand in *La dame aux camélias*, 1852. London debut, 1860; gained fame as untraditional and romantic interpreter of Shakespeare and fascinating star of current high-class melodrama (such as *No Thoroughfare*, by Collins and Dickens). Lessee of the Lyceum Theatre, London, 1862–67. To U.S., 1870 (debut in N.Y.). Unsuccessful ventures as manager: Globe Theatre, Boston, 1870/1; 14th Street Theatre, N.Y., 1872/3. Sporadic acting in N.Y. to 1876 (in French, 1875). His difficult and mercurial personality is said to have counteracted his great gifts. **17. ADELAIDE NEILSON** (real name, Elizabeth Ann Brown; English; 1846–1880). In her lifetime, elaborate legends cloaked the reality of her miserable childhood in the English provinces. Debut at Margate, 1865; London, 1866. Her fresh beauty, allied to genuine acting talent, made her the great Juliet, Rosalind and Viola of her generation (another famous part: the title role of *Amy Robsart*). Visits to all parts of U.S., 1872–74 and 1880. Her farewell performance in N.Y. in 1880 proved unexpectedly to be the last she ever gave.

18

19

20

Three major tragedians. **18. JOHN** Edward **McCUL-LOUGH** (1832–1885); born in Ireland). To U.S., 1847; debut in Philadelphia, 1857. From 1861 to 1867 he worked for Edwin Forrest, from whom he borrowed both rugged style and repertoire (first N.Y. appearance, 1862). Prominent in San Francisco, 1869–77, co-managing with Barrett 1869/70, then on his own (back in N.Y. as star, 1874). Last appearances were in 1884: after N.Y., in Chicago, where his spectacular public breakdown (from paresis) became a cruel American byword. **19. EDWIN** Thomas **BOOTH** (1833–1893; son of Junius Brutus Booth, Sr., no. 1; brother of John Wilkes Booth, no. 11). Most celebrated American tragedian of his day in Shakespeare and high drama. Debut with father, Boston, 1849; N.Y. debut, 1850. California, 1852 (beginning of independent career); to Australia (with Laura Keene), 1854. Back East again, 1857, as "the Hope of the Living Drama." The famous three-brother *Julius Caesar* of November 25, 1864 (N.Y.), was followed on the very next evening by the first of his record-breaking 100 consecutive performances of *Hamlet*. Retired for a year after his brother killed Lincoln. Opened Booth's Theatre, N.Y., 1869, and managed it until 1873 (*Richard II* revival, 1872). In last years, toured with Barrett; N.Y. farewell, March 1891; final farewell, Brooklyn, April 1891. Donated his N.Y. town house to the Players Club, which he founded. **20. LAWRENCE BARRETT** (1838–1891). On stage at age 14; after leads in Boston, made N.Y. debut in 1857. Manager in San Francisco, 1869/70, with McCullough; then, traveling actor/manager, going beyond stock tragedies and injecting fresh plays into his repertoire. A highlight of his career: the major 1883 revival of *Francesca da Rimini* (Skinner in cast). For some time a rival of Booth, he twice joined forces with him, becoming his partner and business manager from 1887 until his death in March 1891 during their N.Y. run.

9

21

22

21. KATE BATEMAN (1842–1917). Began as sensational child actress with sister Ellen; debut, Kentucky, 1846; N.Y., 1849. Taken to London with sister by Barnum, 1851. First adult appearance in N.Y. (without sister), 1860. Enormous success in N.Y. (a success also for the young adapter of the play, Augustin Daly) in *Leah the Forsaken*, 1863. Last N.Y. play (written for her by Tom Taylor): *Mary Warner*, 1869 (role in photo). From 1871 to 1906, only in London (her father managed the Lyceum, where she acted with the young Henry Irving). **22. C**(harles) **W**(alter) **COULDOCK** (1815–1898; born in England). Debut, 1835, London. To N.Y., 1849, in support of Charlotte Cushman, who was then returning from England. The role of his life was in the play *Hazel Kirke* (N.Y., 1880; it had opened in Providence, 1879, as *An Iron Will*). In 1886, acted with Salvini and Booth. Last appearance, 1898, N.Y. in a *Hazel Kirke* revival. **23. FANNY** (Francesca) **JANAUSCHEK** (1829–1904; born in Prague). Debut in Prague at 16. At 19, leading lady in Frankfurt a/M. To U.S. (N.Y.), 1867, acting only in German until 1870. Great touring roles: Meg Merrilies, Lady Macbeth, Mary Stuart. She lost her money in investments, and her popularity waned in the 1890s. In N.Y., 1895, in tawdry melodrama *The Great Diamond Robbery*. Vaudeville, 1898. **24. MRS. D. P. BOWERS** (née Elizabeth Crocker; ca. 1830–1895). N.Y. debut, 1845. Leading lady for the Drews at the Arch Street Theatre, Philadelphia,

1853 ff.; at Walnut Street Theatre in that city, 1857–59. On return from 1861–63 English visit, made her greatest success in *Lady Audley's Secret*. Acted with Booth, 1880, and Salvini, 1886. In first N.Y. production of *Lady Windermere's Fan*, 1893. Last N.Y. appearance, 1895, in *The Transgressor* (Olga Nethersole's American debut). **25. EFFIE** (Euphemia) **ELLSLER** (1854–1942). Daughter of the great Cleveland manager John Ellsler, she was on stage almost from birth and learned her art in his stock company from age 15. Enduring fame, N.Y., 1880, in title role of *Hazel Kirke*. In the 1880s, a traveling star of melodrama. Very long film career began 1910. Other important N.Y. stage appearances: *We Are Seven* (1913) and (last play in N.Y.) *The Bat* (1920–22). In 1928 she acted on a Los Angeles stage in *The Goose Hangs High*. **26. ROSE EYTINGE** (1835–1911). Amateur, Brooklyn, 1852; professional debut shortly thereafter in Syracuse. N.Y. debut, 1863, at Laura Keene's Theatre. Supported Booth, 1864 and 1866. With Boston as base, a member of the Wallack-Davenport acting combination, 1865 ff. Leading lady at Wallack's Theatre, N.Y., 1867–69. As lead at the Union Square Theatre, N.Y., 1873 ff., appeared in: *Led Astray* (1873); *The Two Orphans* (1874); and her greatest success, *Rose Michel* (1875; starring tour later; role shown in photo). Own company, early 1890s; still active 1907.

27

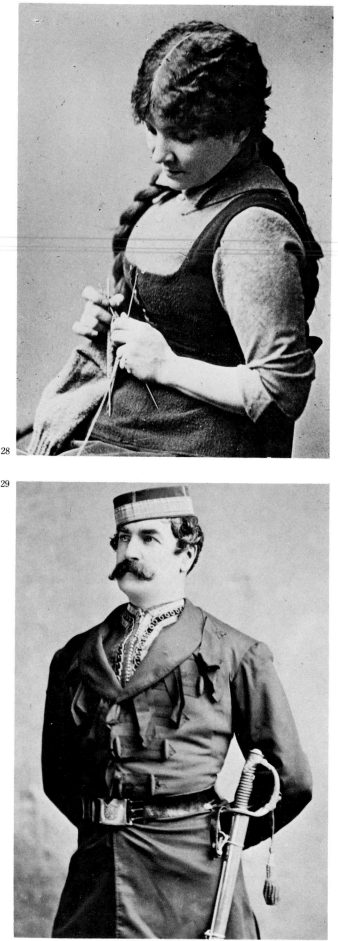

28

29

27. AGNES BOOTH (née Marion Land Rookes; 1843–1910; born in Australia; the second of her three husbands was Junius Brutus Booth, Jr., Edwin's older brother). Debut at age 14 in Sydney. U.S. debut in San Francisco, 1858, in Mrs. John Wood's company. In San Francisco till 1865, then to N.Y. From 1866 to 1873, leading lady at the Boston Theatre, specializing in emotional French plays. Star tour, 1874–76; then, lead in three eminent N.Y. stock companies: Union Square Theatre, 1877/8 (in *A Celebrated Case*, 1878); Abbey's Park Theatre, 1878 ff. (in Gilbert's *Engaged*, 1879); Madison Square Theatre, 1881–91 (in *Esmeralda*, 1881, and *Jim the Penman*, 1886). Retired 1897, but made a N.Y. appearance in 1903. **28. KATE CLAXTON** (1848–1924; real surname Cone). Debut, 1869, Chicago; N.Y., 1870, at Daly's. After 2-1/2 years with Daly, she joined the Union Square Company, eventually succeeding Rose Eytinge as leading lady; here she enjoyed her greatest triumph in *The Two Orphans* (1874; role in photo), which she played ever after (she acquired the rights to the play and D. W. Griffith had to deal with her when making his film version, *Orphans of the Storm*). Star from 1876 (she was playing the Brooklyn Theatre that year when the disastrous fire occurred). Later she and her husband produced plays in N.Y. Retirement as actress, 1911. **29. LESTER WALLACK** (real given name, John Johnstone: 1819 or 1820–1888). His father, James William Wallack, Sr., founded Wallack's Theatre, N.Y., in 1852. Lester, born in N.Y., made his debut in London in 1846; N.Y. debut, 1847 (as "J. Lester"). A great manager (he took over the theater when his father died in 1864, and made it the premier stock house in the country), he was also an eminent actor in Shakespeare, the classics and current British imports, especially Tom Robertson's "cup-and-saucer" plays. Acting highlights: *The Romance of a Poor Young Man* (1860); *Rosedale* (1863); *Ours* (1866). Acted to 1886, managed to 1887.

31

32

30. E(dward) **A**(skew) **SOTHERN** (English; 1826–1881; father of E. H. Sothern, no. 87). Stock in England from ca. 1849. U.S. debut in Boston, 1852 (up to 1856, used the name Douglas Stuart). With Laura Keene in her Baltimore venture, 1853. At Wallack's, N.Y., 1854. In 1858, back with Keene (in N.Y.), he made one of the hits of the century as Lord Dundreary (role in photo) in *Our American Cousin* (he played the part, and its spinoffs, for many years). Back in England, 1861–71. Later big parts in U.S.: *David Garrick* (1873; he had done it in London, 1864) and *The Crushed Tragedian* (1877; earlier in England). To England again, 1880. **31. MARY** Antoinette **ANDERSON** (1859–1940; after her marriage in 1890, Mrs. Antonio de Navarro). Debut in Louisville, 1875, as Juliet; N.Y., 1877. Beautiful and graceful, she quickly won fame in classical and modern poetic drama. In London, 1883–85, she captured English hearts (created main role in Gilbert's *Comedy and Tragedy*, 1884). Last N.Y. appearance, 1888 (*The Winter's Tale*); last appearance of all, Washington, D.C., 1889. Retired to marry, then lived in England. During World War I, she made a few appearances for charity. Co-author (unnamed) with Robert Hichens of the 1911 play derived from his novel *The Garden of Allah*. **32. WILLIAM** Jermyn **FLORENCE** (real name, Bernard Conlin; 1831–1891). Debut, 1849, in Virginia; N.Y., 1850. In 1853 ff., appeared in comic Irish characters along with his wife (in emulation of her sister and brother-in-law, Mr. and Mrs. Barney Williams), but his great talent soon impelled him to attempt nobler things. Although essentially a comedian, he could play such parts as Obenreizer in *No Thoroughfare* and Bob Brierly in *The Ticket-of-Leave Man* (U.S. creation, 1863). He was the first to produce Robertson's *Caste* in the U.S., 1867. The greatest success of his life was in the political comedy *The Mighty Dollar* (1875); his last great role was Sir Lucius O'Trigger in an 1889 all-star *Rivals* revival.

33

On this page and the following: four major stars of comedy of the late 19th century. **33. JOHN T. RAYMOND** (real name, John O'Brien; 1836–1887; son-in-law of Rose Eytinge, no. 26). Debut, 1853, Rochester; then, active in Philadelphia, Baltimore and the South. N.Y. debut, 1860. In 1862/3, he was in Laura Keene's company, replacing Joseph Jefferson. In 1867/8, in England with E. A. Sothern. In 1869, in San Francisco with Barrett and McCullough. In 1871, with Lotta. His real breakthrough was in the role of Colonel Sellers in *The Gilded Age* (from 1873; N.Y., 1874); none of his other plays was as successful. Appearances in N.Y. at least to 1885 (*In Chancery*, by Pinero). **34. STUART ROBSON** (real name, Henry Robson Stuart; 1836–1903). As a boy in Baltimore he did home acting with the young Booths. His professional debut was in that city in 1852 in a theater managed by John E. Owens. His N.Y. debut was with Laura Keene in 1862. After years in Philadelphia, New Orleans and Boston, he joined the Union Square Theatre stock company in N.Y. in 1871. In 1877 he appeared with W. H. Crane in *Our Boarding-House*. They made such a hit together that they remained acting partners until 1889, when they decided they could earn more money separately (highlights of partnership: revival of *The Comedy of Errors*, 1878, and *The Henrietta*, 1887–89). Robson's last N.Y. appearance was in *Oliver Goldsmith*, 1899.

34

35

36

35. JOHN E(dmond) **OWENS** (1823–1886; born in England). He came to the U.S. in 1828, and made his debut in Philadelphia, 1840, with the comedian W. E. Burton. N.Y. debut with the comedian John Brougham, 1850. In 1853 he gave illustrated lectures on an ascent of Mont Blanc (plagiarism of a London entertainment). His greatest success was as the Yankee farmer Solon Shingle in a revival of *The People's Lawyer* (he first acted this in 1856; N.Y., 1864). A tireless trouper, he acted in N.Y. and elsewhere till almost the end of his life. **36. W**(illiam) **H**(enry) **CRANE** (1845–1928). Debut, 1863, Utica; in popular concert and comic-opera troupes for many years (first N.Y. appearance, 1872; in first version of the musical burlesque *Evangeline*, N.Y., 1874). Member of stock companies in Chicago, San Francisco and N.Y., 1874–76. For his magnificent partnership with Stuart Robson, 1877–89, see no. 34. As a lone star thereafter, he was a loyal patron of American comic playwrights, though none of his vehicles was of great significance until *David Harum* in 1900. His last N.Y. play was *The New Henrietta* (1913), with Douglas Fairbanks in the cast.

Four outstanding female personalities. **37. MRS. JOHN WOOD** (née Matilda Charlotte Vining; English; 1831–1915). This sprightly comedienne and manager made her debut in Brighton in 1841. In 1854 she came to the U.S., specially engaged for the opening show at the new Boston Theatre. She first acted in N.Y. in 1856; in San Francisco, 1858. In 1859 she was the original Tilly Slowboy in Boucicault's *Dot* at the Winter Garden, N.Y. By 1860 she starred, and from 1863 to 1866 she ran Mrs. John Wood's Olympic Theatre in N.Y. Afterwards, she was chiefly active in London (some U.S. appearances in the early 1870s), managing the St. James's and the Court and acting to at least 1903. **38. MAGGIE** (Margaret) **MITCHELL** (1832–1918). This diminutive actress kept playing girlish and pure characters for 40 years. Coming from an acting family, she made her debut in N.Y. in 1851. She became a touring star in the 1853/4 season. Her most successful play, which she used for over a quarter of a century, was *Fanchon the Cricket* (1860; N.Y., 1862). She retired, a wealthy woman, in 1891. Her son Julian Mitchell was a topnotch director of musical comedy and revue, working for Weber & Fields, Ziegfeld and others. **39. ANNIE PIXLEY** (ca. 1856–1893). Born in Brooklyn, but moved to San Francisco as a small child. Acting in San Francisco by 1876; in that year she visited Australia. Supported Joseph Jefferson when he did *Rip Van Winkle* in San Francisco in 1878. During the nationwide *H.M.S. Pinafore* craze of 1879, she left California to try her luck in the East, and found lasting success with the play *M'liss* (N.Y., 1880 and repeatedly thereafter), based on Bret Harte.

37

38

39

40. LOTTA (Charlotte Mignon Crabtree; 1847–1924). Born in N.Y., she moved to California in 1853. Coached as a singing, dancing and banjo-playing actress by the notorious Lola Montez, she began entertaining in mining camps about 1854 and was appearing in tailor-made plays by 1858. Enormously popular in the West, she failed in her first N.Y. foray, 1864, but was successful even in that citadel in 1867 in *Little Nell and the Marchioness*. All her plays were merely personal appearances built around her own girlish charm and assorted musical talents, but the public loved her and she was very rich when she retired in 1890. Wise real-estate investments made her a highly prominent citizen of Boston in her later years.

41

42

43

41. **HELENA MODJESKA** (actually, Modrzejewska; née Opid; Polish; 1840–1909). She had her own small traveling company by 1861 and was the toast of Warsaw by 1868, but intrigues drove her from Poland in 1876. In California she was encouraged by Booth to act in English, and she made her American debut in San Francisco in 1877 (N.Y., same year). She soon became nationally famous for her refinement and charm in Shakespeare and high-class modern plays. Her 1883 Nora in Louisville may have been the first Ibsen in the U.S.; in 1894 she was the first American Magda in Sudermann's play. She received a retirement benefit in N.Y. in 1905, but toured in 1906. **42.** Dame **ELLEN** Alice **TERRY** (English; 1847–1928). The most revered English actress of her day, she began acting with Charles Kean in 1856. She first appeared opposite Irving in 1867, then became his regular partner from 1878 to 1902. Together they made triumphal tours of the U.S. between 1883 and 1902. She continued to appear in noteworthy productions (some in association with her son Gordon Craig). Jubilee celebration, 1906; U.S. tour, 1907; afterwards, much lecturing. Made a DBE in 1925. **43.** Sir **HENRY IRVING** (real name, John Henry Brodribb; English; 1838–1905). First English actor to be knighted (1895). Acting debut, 1856; in London briefly, 1859; permanently, 1866. Began appearing at the Lyceum Theatre, 1871, under management of H. L. Bateman (father of Kate Bateman); in 1878 took over that house, which he made a theatrical pilgrimage site. For his U.S. tours, see no. 42. Acted to the day of his death.

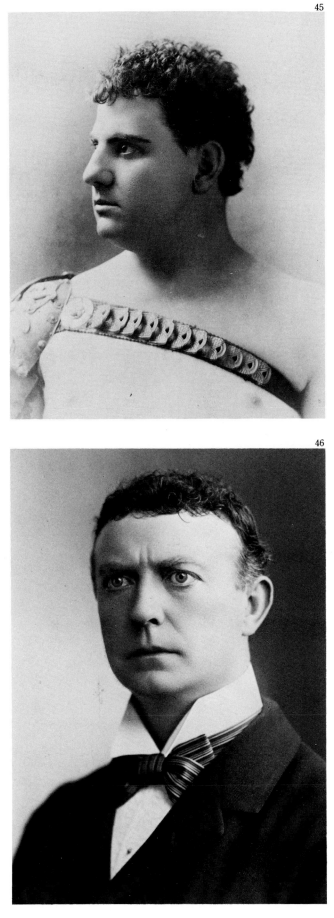

44. WALKER WHITESIDE (1869–1942). Debut, 1884, Chicago. First in N.Y., 1893, with his own Shakespearean company. Chiefly a touring star, he made numerous N.Y. appearances up to 1932, often portraying exotic types: *The Melting Pot* (1907); *Typhoon* (1912); *Mr. Wu* (1914); *The Hindu* (1922); *The Arabian* (1927). Still active, 1935. **45. ROBERT L. DOWNING** (1857–1944). Debut in his native Washington, D.C., 1876; leading man there, 1880. Tours with Mary Anderson, 1880–84 (his first N.Y. appearance, 1880), and Joseph Jefferson, 1884–86. From 1886, a star, specializing in Shakespeare and other heroic roles. After his retirement in 1908, he became a preacher. **46. ROBERT B. MANTELL** (1854–1928; born in Scotland). Debut in England, 1874. First U.S. visit, 1875; second, 1878 (acted with Modjeska). After his 1883 U.S. tour, in which he successfully partnered Fanny Davenport in *Fedora*, he stayed on, achieving stardom in 1886. A strong, magnetic actor in Shakespeare and high romance, he was active to at least 1924 (Chicago).

47

47. HERBERT KELCEY (real surname, Lamb; 1855–1917; born in England). Debut, 1877, Brighton; London, 1880; U.S. (N.Y.), 1882. Acted at Wallack's, the Madison Square Theatre and, 1887–96, the Lyceum (leading man from 1888). In 1897 he formed an acting partnership with Effie Shannon that lasted, on and off, till 1915. Their greatest success together was *The Moth and the Flame* (1898). In 1916 he was in *Pollyanna*. **48. EFFIE SHANNON** (1867–1954). Debut as child with McCullough in Boston. N.Y., 1886, with Mantell. In Daly's company, 1887–89, then (to 1893) ingenue at the Lyceum. For partnership with Kelcey, see no. 47. Outstanding plays of her long career: *Widowers' Houses* (1907); *Heartbreak House* (1920); *Detour* (1921); *The Truth About Blaydes* (1932); *The Wingless Victory* (1936); *Morning's at Seven* (1939). In 1941 ff. she toured in *Arsenic and Old Lace*. **49. MRS. G**(eorge) **H**(enry) **GILBERT** (née Anne Jane Hartley; 1821–1904; born in England). Dancer in London at age 12. She and her husband, also a dancer (died 1866), came to the U.S. in 1850, appearing in Midwest stock companies. She began regular acting only later. N.Y., 1864, with Mrs. John Wood. Big N.Y. success, 1867, in *Caste*. From 1869 to 1899, much beloved "first old lady" in Augustin Daly's prestigious N.Y. company. Later with Charles Frohman. Last appearance in *Granny* (1904).

49

48

Three stars associated with Augustin Daly. **50. ADA REHAN** (Crehan; 1860–1916; born in Ireland). To U.S. at age 5. Acting by 1873 with her sister and brother-in-law, Kate and Oliver Doud Byron (first in N.Y. with them, 1875). Acted many roles, including leads, in Philadelphia, Louisville, Albany and Baltimore before joining Daly's, N.Y., in 1879. Almost at once she became leading woman, playing everything from frothy farce to Shakespeare: first Rosalind, 1889; first Lady Teazle, 1891 (role in photo). Great success on Daly's visits to London, beginning in 1884. In 1894, she formally became the star of the company. After her manager's death in 1899, she retired for a year. In *Sweet Nell of Old Drury* (1900). Full retirement, 1905. **51. CLARA MORRIS** (actually, Morrison; 1846–1925; born in Canada). Started as dancer in Cleveland, 1859; then in Ellsler's stock company there. With Daly in N.Y., 1870–73, making a startling hit with her sincere emotionality (*Article 47*, 1872). For the next few years, at the Union Square (*Camille*, 1874; *Miss Multon*, 1876), then stardom (*The New Magdalen* revival, 1882). After 1896, vaudeville. Last regular N.Y. play, 1904; active elsewhere to at least 1906; N.Y. testimonial, 1909. **52. FANNY DAVENPORT** (1850–1898; born in England; daughter of E. L. Davenport, no. 6). To U.S., 1854; in N.Y. show with parents, 1857. Regular N.Y. debut, 1862. With Daly (soon as lead) from 1869 to 1875, when her work in *Pique* gained her star status. Most famous in her later career as emotional U.S. interpreter of Bernhardt roles: *Fedora* (1883); *La Tosca* (1888); *Cleopatra* (1890); *Gismonda* (1894).

53

54

55

53. JULIA ARTHUR (née Ida Lewis; 1869–1950; born in Canada). Debut, 1883, with Daniel Bandmann; in N.Y. with him (as Ida Lewis), 1886. Back in N.Y., 1891 ff., at the Union Square (*Lady Windermere's Fan*, 1893). In the 1895/6 season, with Irving in London and U.S. Star in U.S. from 1897; wealthy marriage allowed her to mount Shakespeare and classics sumptuously. Retired, 1900–14; back in N.Y., 1915. Last N.Y., 1921, as Lionel Barrymore's Lady Macbeth. Active until at least the 1924/5 season. **54. MRS. LESLIE CARTER** (née Caroline Louise Dudley; 1862–1937). Turning to the stage after a sensational society divorce, she placed herself in David Belasco's hands. Mute role, 1887. N.Y., 1890. Her great Belasco successes included: *The Heart of Maryland* (1895); *Zaza* (1898; N.Y., 1899); and *Du Barry* (1901). She left Belasco, 1906. Retired, 1917–21. Triumphal return in Maugham's *The Circle* (1921). Last N.Y. play: all-star *She Stoops to Conquer*, 1928. Revival of *The Circle* in Hollywood, 1934. **55. ROSE COGHLAN** (1851–1932; born in England). Debut, 1868, in Greenwich, Scotland; London, 1869. To U.S., 1871 (debut at Wallack's, N.Y., 1872). England again, 1873–77; then back as leading lady at Wallack's, 1877–85 (and 1887/8): in *Diplomacy* (1878), *Forget-Me-Not* (1880), *The Silver King* (1883). Star, 1888. In *A Woman of No Importance* (1894; her own production). Vaudeville, 1898. Unsuccessful later career although admired by N.Y. critics. Last N.Y. play: *Deburau* (1920).

56

57

58

56. MAURICE BARRYMORE (real name, Herbert Blythe; 1847–1905; born in India; father of Ethel, Lionel and John Barrymore, nos. 74–76). Champion amateur boxer in England before acting in provincial stock. U.S. debut, 1875, Boston; with Daly, N.Y., same year. Leading man at Wallack's, 1879; at Union Square, 1888–93 (*Lady Windermere's Fan*, 1893). In *The Heart of Maryland* (1895). Often worked as romantic leading man to star actresses: Modjeska (1882–86), Lillie Langtry (1887/8), Mrs. Fiske (1898/9). One of the first major actors in vaudeville (from 1897). Was married to Georgiana Drew, daughter of Mrs. John Drew, from 1876 to her death in 1893. Suffered mental collapse, 1901. 57. JAMES K(eteltas) HACKETT (1869–1926; born in Canada; son of James H. Hackett, no. 7; married, 1897–1910, to Mary Mannering, no. 92). Debut, Philadelphia, 1892; N.Y., same year. At Daly's and Union Square and with Lotta before taking leads at the Lyceum (from 1895; succeeded Sothern in *The Prisoner of Zenda*, 1896). Star, 1898; *Rupert of Hentzau*, that year. In *The Walls of Jericho* (1905). Later, important producer at Hackett Theatre, N.Y. (earlier, Fields'). *Macbeth* tour with Viola Allen, 1915/6. Last N.Y. play, 1919. 58. JAMES O'NEILL (1847–1920; born in Ireland; father of Eugene O'Neill). To U.S., 1854. Debut in Cincinnati, ca. 1865. Active especially in the Midwest and San Francisco (first in N.Y., 1875). The New Testament *Passion Play* (1878), a California success, was banned in N.Y. Turning point of career: a revival of *The Count of Monte Cristo* at Booth's in N.Y., 1883—so loved by the public that O'Neill could hardly play anything else until 1891 (then, elaborate revival, 1900 ff.). In N.Y. in later years: *The White Sister* (1909); *Joseph and His Brethren* (1913); *The Wanderer* (1917).

59. E(dmund) M(ilton) HOLLAND (1848–1913; son of the popular comedian George Holland, whose funeral led to the affinity of actors for The Little Church Around the Corner in N.Y.). On stage, 1855; real debut, 1866. A polished character comedian, he was in Wallack's company, 1867–79; at the Madison Square Theatre, 1882–90; with Charles Frohman, 1897–1902. Then, with Viola Allen (1902/3; *The Eternal City*), Kyrle Bellew (1903/4; *Raffles*), Otis Skinner, Eleanor Robson and Wilton Lackaye. In the stock company of the prestigious New Theatre in N.Y., 1909–12. **60. JAMES A. HERNE** (real surname, Ahearn; 1839–1901; father of Chrystal Herne, no. 143). Debut, 1859, Troy (there to 1861). Baltimore, 1861–64; made opening address at Ford's Theatre in Washington, 1864. In 1866 ff., with the Western sisters (N.Y., 1871). Later, as playwright and actor, a pioneer in realism and a warmhearted interpreter of American rural life: *Margaret Fleming* (1888; an early "problem play"); *Shore Acres* (1892); *Griffith Davenport* (1899; role in photo); *Sag Harbour* (1899). **61. WILTON LACKAYE** (1862–1932). Debut with Barrett in N.Y., 1883. Worked with Fanny Davenport, Rose Coghlan, Daly, Kate Claxton and others. Fame as Svengali in first dramatization of *Trilby* (N.Y., 1895; also in the revivals of 1905, 1915 and 1921). In *Children of the Ghetto*, 1899. Steadily active in N.Y. plays to 1930.

64

62. RICHARD MANSFIELD (1854–1907; born in Germany, grew up in England). Began in English musical entertainments and comic opera; 3 years in provincial Gilbert and Sullivan companies (Major General in copyright premiere of *The Pirates of Penzance*, Paignton, 1879). U.S. debut (still in comic opera), 1882. Breakthrough as highly dramatic and versatile actor at the Union Square (*A Parisian Romance*, 1883). As a star (from 1886), emulated Irving and Tree as a "total" actor/manager: *Dr. Jekyll and Mr. Hyde* (1887); *Beau Brummel* (1890); *Arms and the Man* (1894; first Shaw in U.S.); *The Devil's Disciple* (1897); *Cyrano de Bergerac* (1898); *Henry V* (1900); *Peer Gynt* (1906).   **63. NAT**(haniel) **C**(arr) **GOODWIN** (Jr.; 1857–1919). Gifted light comedian who made some excursions into plays of heroic pathos; one of his wives was Maxine Elliott, no. 103. Debut, Boston, 1874, as protégé of Stuart Robson; N.Y. (in variety), 1875. Long in variety and "burlesque" (an early form of musical comedy) before switching to regular farce in 1881 and to drama in 1888. Highlights of career: *In Mizzoura* (1893); Sir Lucius O'Trigger in an all-star *Rivals* (1895); *Nathan Hale* (1898); *When We Were Twenty-one* (1900); *The Merchant of Venice* (1901). Last N.Y. play: *Why Marry?* (1917; first Pulitzer Prize play).   **64. DENMAN THOMPSON** (1833–1911). One of the numerous 19th-century stars nationally famous for a single play. On stage from ca. 1850 (lecturer for George Catlin's Indian show in N.Y., 1851). His one-act variety play *The Female Bathers* became the longer *Joshua Whitcomb* (1875, Pittsburgh; 1878, N.Y.). In Boston, 1886 (N.Y., 1887), it finally emerged as the rural comedy-with-songs *The Old Homestead*, which he played for the rest of his life.

65. **ELSIE** Anderson **DE WOLFE** (1865–1950). A leading high-society amateur actress (performances in London and N.Y., 1885), she went professional in 1891 after losing her fortune. After years at the Union Square and Charles Frohman's Empire Theatre, she left the stage in 1904 to concentrate on interior designing. In 1926 she married Sir Charles Mendl and became the famous Lady Mendl. 66. **ROBERT C. HILLIARD** (1857–1927). Beginning as a serious amateur in Brooklyn, 1880, he made his professional debut in a company of his own (Brooklyn, then N.Y., 1886). Important plays: *Blue Jeans* (1890; he was saved from the famous buzzsaw); *The Girl of the Golden West* (1905; as the original romantic bandit, Dick Johnson); *A Fool There Was* (1908). Last N.Y. play, 1917. 67. **PHOEBE DAVIES** (or Davis; 1864–1912; born in Wales). Came to U.S., 1871. Debut San Francisco, 1880; enormous range of roles in stock there. With her local leading man, Joseph R. Grismer, whom she married, she formed an acting organization that eventually roamed the country in highly popular "heart" plays: *The New South* (N.Y. debut, 1892); *Humanity* (1894; N.Y., 1895); and especially *'Way Down East* (1897), which was just about her only vehicle until at least 1909 (later filmed by Griffith).

68. Olga Nethersole and Hamilton Revelle in *Sapho*, 1900. **OLGA** Isabel **NETHERSOLE** (English; 1863–1951). She made her debut in England, 1887; in the London West End, 1888. After acting with John Hare, 1889–93, she took over the Court Theatre on her own in 1894. In that year she made her U.S. debut in N.Y., in a season of highly emotional romantic dramas, her forte. In all, she made 10 U.S. tours up to 1913, her last full year of acting (one London performance, 1923), starring in such plays as: *Carmen* (1895); *The Second Mrs. Tanqueray*

(1899); and the very daring *Sapho* (1900). Arthur **HAMILTON REVELLE** (1872–1958; born on Gibraltar). He made his debut with Daly, N.Y., 1888. In England, mid-1890s. Supported Nethersole in her 1899/1900 U.S. tour (and in 1905/6), then became a Belasco player: *Du Barry* (1901); *The Rose of the Rancho* (1906). Later N.Y. plays included: *Kismet* (as the evil wazir); *Fair and Warmer* (1915); *Mis' Nelly of N'Orleans* (1919; with Mrs. Fiske); and *Captain Applejack* (1921; his last).

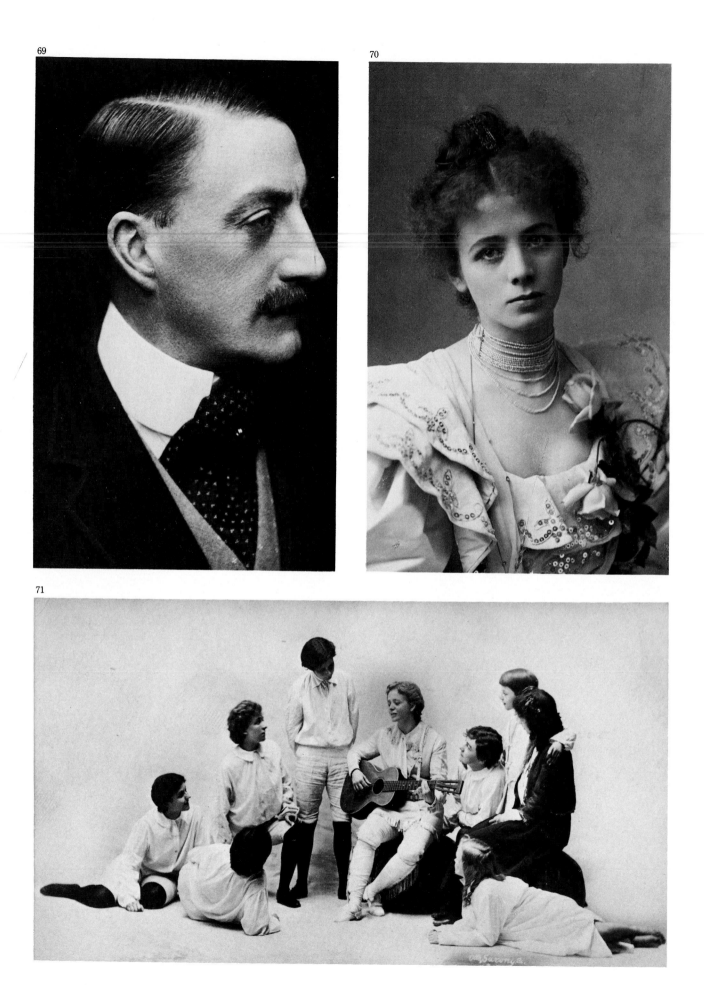

69

70

71

28

69. JOHN DREW (Jr.; 1853–1927; son of Louisa Drew, no. 8: uncle of the Barrymores, nos. 74–76). Debut at his mother's Arch Street Theatre in Philadelphia, 1873. Great success at Daly's, N.Y., 1875–92, as lead opposite Ada Rehan. From 1892, a Charles Frohman star in a long series of suave British high-society imports: *The Liars* (1898); *The Tyranny of Tears* (1899); *His House in Order* (1906); etc. Brilliant in Maugham's *The Circle* (1921). Died during the 1927 touring revival of *Trelawny of the "Wells."* **70 & 71. MAUDE ADAMS** (1872–1953). Carried on stage at 9 months in Salt Lake City, where her mother, Annie Adams Kiskadden, played in stock. Much child acting, especially in San Francisco. In 1888, she joined E. H. Sothern's company as it came through on tour, first playing N.Y. in that year. After success in *A Midnight Bell* in 1889, she was engaged by Charles Frohman and became John Drew's leading lady for 5 years. Star in *The Little Minister* (1897; role in photo 70), and then continued to be Barrie's leading U.S. interpreter: *Quality Street* (1901); *Peter Pan* (1905; her most famous role; photo 71); *What Every Woman Knows* (1908); *A Kiss for Cinderella* (1916). Memorable Juliet, 1899. In two major masculine roles by Rostand: *L'Aiglon* (1900) and *Chantecler* (1911). Retired, 1918–31.

Toured in *The Merchant of Venice*, 1931; did *Twelfth Night* in Maine, 1934. **72. MINNIE MADDERN FISKE** (Mrs. Fiske; née Marie Augusta Davey; 1864–1932). Years of stage drudgery from age 3 in her family's fly-by-night troupe. Acted as child with Laura Keene, McCullough, J. K. Emmet (first N.Y., 1870). Star, 1882. After marrying publisher Harrison Grey Fiske in 1890, she retired for 3 years, then emerged as a serious, independent and original actress/director with great technical resources. In: *A Doll's House* (1894); *Tess of the D'Urbervilles* (1897); *Becky Sharp* (1899); *Hedda Gabler* (1903); *Leah Kleschna* (1904); *The New York Idea* (1906); *Salvation Nell* (1908); *Mrs. Bumpstead-Leigh* (1911); and an endless string of worthy plays. Last N.Y. appearance, 1930. Last of all: Chicago, 1931, interrupted by fatal illness. **73. NANCE O'NEIL** (real name, Gertrude Lamson; 1874–1965). Debut, 1893, San Francisco; Broadway, 1896. After attaining stardom in 1898, principally toured in repertory all over U.S. and world, specializing in high-quality 19th-century and modern roles. Relatively infrequent N.Y. appearances included *Night in the House* (*The Old Ladies*; 1935) and her last, as Queen Margaret in José Ferrer's *Richard III* (1946–48).

74

75

The Barrymores, America's most famous theatrical siblings, were the children of Maurice Barrymore (no. 56); to a large extent, they were raised by their maternal grandmother, Mrs. John Drew (no. 8), who indoctrinated them in stage ways at a tender age. **74. LIONEL BAR-RYMORE** (1878–1954). Acted with his grandmother in Kansas City, 1893, and N.Y., 1894. In 1897 he was with Nance O'Neil; in 1900, in *Sag Harbour* with Herne. For two seasons he supported his maternal uncle, John Drew. Chief plays: *Peter Ibbetson* (1917); *The Copperhead* (1918; his greatest personal stage success); *The Jest* (1919); and the disastrous 1921 *Macbeth*. Last N.Y. play, 1925; then, illustrious film career (begun in 1909). **75. JOHN BARRYMORE** (1882–1942). Appeared at a benefit, 1901. Real debut in Chicago, 1903, with Nance O'Neil; N.Y., same year. In one musical: *A Stubborn Cinderella* (1908; N.Y., 1909). Emerged as gifted juvenile and matinee idol: *The Fortune Hunter* (1909). First serious role in *Kick In* (1914). The fame he gained in *Justice* (1916) was nurtured by: *Peter Ibbetson* (1917); *Redemption* (1918); *The Jest* (1919); and *Richard III* (1920). Pinnacle of career: the much-lauded *Hamlet* (1922; brought to London with great success,

1925). Afterwards, important film career progressively marred by self-indulgence and dissipation. Pathetic return to the stage in *My Dear Children* (Chicago, 1939; N.Y., 1940). **76. ETHEL BARRYMORE** (1879–1959). Acted with her grandmother in Montreal, 1894; in N.Y., same year, with her uncle John Drew. In England, 1897/8, including tour with Henry Irving. Stardom, N.Y., 1901, in *Captain Jinks of the Horse Marines*. Highlights of the next two decades: *The Silver Box* (1907); *Lady Frederick* (1908); *Mid-Channel* (1910); *Our Mrs. Mc-Chesney* (1915); *Déclassée* (1919; one of her biggest hits and typical of the society drama in which she excelled). Her Juliet of 1922 (same season as Jane Cowl's successful production) was a setback. Ethel Barrymore Theatre, N.Y., opened 1928. The 1930s, in which her career declined, included a blackface role in *Scarlet Sister Mary* (1930) and a stint with the Civic Repertory Company (1934). Grand comeback in *The Corn Is Green* (1940). Then, renewal of film career (Oscar for *None But the Lonely Heart*, 1944). In a revival of Philip Barry's *The Joyous Season* on the Chicago stage, 1946. TV appearance as late as 1956.

76

77

78

79

77. HENRIETTA Foster **CROSMAN** (1861–1944). Debut, 1883, N.Y. Tours with Downing and others. At Lyceum, 1890; with Charles Frohman, 1892–94. Star, 1900, in *Mistress Nell*. In *Sweet Kitty Bellairs* (1903). In 1916, in *The Merry Wives of Windsor*, with Viola Allen and J. K. Hackett, and then with Sir Herbert Tree. In *Children of the Moon* (1923). Last N.Y. play, 1929; last stage work, 1939. **78. WILLIAM** Hooker **GILLETTE** (1853–1937). Scion of a distinguished political family, he ran away to act. Debut in New Orleans, 1875; in N.Y., same year. Gained fame acting in plays of which he was author or adaptor: *The Professor* (1881); *The Private Secretary* (1884); *Held by the Enemy* (1886); *Too Much Johnson* (1894); *Secret Service* (great Civil War melodrama, first done in Philadelphia, 1895, with Maurice Barrymore in lead role; then, revised, in N.Y., 1896, with Gillette); and—his most famous role and play—*Sherlock Holmes* (1899; earliest dramatization; revived by him up to 1931). Major parts in plays by others: *The Admirable Crichton* (1903); *Samson* (1908); *Dear Brutus* (1918). Last N.Y. play: revival of *Three Wise Fools* (1937). Famous for his quiet, "natural" acting. His domain on the Connecticut River is now open to the public. **79. ELEANOR ROBSON** (1879–1979; born in England; daughter of the actress Madge Carr Cook, the original stage Mrs. Wiggs). To U.S., 1885; debut in San Francisco, 1897. N.Y., 1900, in *Arizona* (done earlier in Chicago). Later plays: *In a Balcony* (1900; with Skinner); *A Gentleman of France* (1901; N.Y., 1902; with Bellew; role in photo); *Merely Mary Ann* (1903); *Nurse Marjorie* (1906). Shaw wanted her to create Major Barbara, but she was tied to contracts. Last stage (and last N.Y.), 1909; retired to marry August Belmont. Later well known as founder of the Metropolitan Opera Guild.

80

81

82

Three great David Belasco stars. **80. DAVID WARFIELD** (1866–1951). Debut in San Francisco, ca. 1888; N.Y., 1890, doing a monologue. Up to the end of the century, Jewish comic in musicals, including 3 years with Weber & Fields. From 1901, Belasco star in four sentimental plays that were toured and revived for years and years: *The Auctioneer* (1901); *The Music Master* (1904); *A Grand Army Man* (1907); and *The Return of Peter Grimm* (1911). Last N.Y. appearance as Shylock in *The Merchant of Venice* (1922; on road to 1924). **81. BLANCHE BATES** (1873–1941). Daughter of West Coast actors, she went on stage 1894 in San Francisco, playing a wide range of leading roles in local stock. N.Y. debut, 1897, with Daly. Important roles, 1899, in *The Musketeers* (with James O'Neill) and *Children of the Ghetto*. Then, the Belasco years, with lead roles in such plays as: *Madame Butterfly* (1900); *Under Two Flags* (1901); *The Darling of the Gods* (1902); and *The Girl of the Golden West* (1905; role in photo). Greatest later success: *The Famous Mrs. Fair* (1919). In 1926, with Margaret Anglin on the West Coast. No acting for 7 years; then, in 1933, a tour and her last N.Y. play: *The Lake* (in which Katharine Hepburn "ran the gamut of emotions from A to B"). **82. FRANCES** Grant **STARR** (1886–1973). Began in Albany stock, 1901; in N.Y. stock, same year. Real Broadway debut, 1906; later that year she took over a role in Belasco's *The Music Master* (with Warfield) and won the lead in the same producer's *The Rose of the Rancho*. Other Belasco hits: *The Easiest Way* (1909) and *Marie Odile* (1915). Later N.Y. plays included: *The Lake* (1933); *Moor Born* (1934; as Charlotte Brontë); *Claudia* (1941); and (her last) *The Ladies of the Corridor* (1953).

83

84

85

83. HENRY MILLER (real name, John Pegge; 1859–1926; born in England). To Canada at age 11. Debut, Toronto, 1878; N.Y., 1880, with Adelaide Neilson. After work with Modjeska, Daly, Minnie Maddern, Clara Morris and others, he was leading juvenile at the Lyceum, 1887–89, and leading man at the Empire, 1893–96 (first U.S. John Worthing in *The Importance of Being Earnest*, 1895). Star, 1897. In *The Only Way* (1899). Important work with Margaret Anglin, 1903 ff., especially *The Great Divide* (1906). Henry Miller's Theatre opened in N.Y., 1918. In *The Famous Mrs. Fair* (1919) and *Pasteur* (1923). Active to the end, he appeared on Broadway in 1926. **84. MARGARET ANGLIN** (1876–1958; born in Canada). Spotted by Charles Frohman in his acting school, she made her debut in N.Y., 1894. After seasons with O'Neill, Sothern and Mansfield (his Roxane in *Cyrano*, 1898), she first teamed up with Henry Miller in *The Only Way* (1899; for further work with Miller, see no. 83). Leading lady at Empire Theatre, 1900–03. From 1910, interested in ancient Greek plays, which she produced at the Greek Theatre in Berkeley and elsewhere. Shakespeare tours, 1913/4 (N.Y., 1914). Greek plays, N.Y., 1918 and 1921. Many tours as pioneer of the "new stagecraft" (imaginative settings based on European experiments). Last N.Y. play, 1936; still active, 1943. **85. FRANK J. KEENAN** (1858–1929). Amateur in Boston, 1876. Much stock and repertory. N.Y., 1891, in an extravaganza; in comedy-with-songs *A Milk White Flag* (1894). Later, vigorous actor of high-class melodrama: *The Christian* (1898); *The Girl of the Golden West* (1905; original sheriff, Jack Rance); *The Warrens of Virginia* (1907). Last N.Y. play, 1914. Silent film work. Chicago play, 1927.

86

87

88

86. Peter Christopher **ARNOLD DALY** (1875–1927). Debut, 1892. Toured with Julia Marlowe, Nat Goodwin, Amelia Bingham, Elsie de Wolfe, Arthur Byron. N.Y., 1895. Star, 1903. From that year, chief early exponent of Shaw in U.S., introducing *Candida, The Man of Destiny, How He Lied to Her Husband, You Never Can Tell, John Bull's Other Island* and *Mrs. Warren's Profession*. In 1920, N.Y., in Cohan's comedy *The Tavern*. Last N.Y. play, 1921. **87.** **E**(dward) **H**(ugh) **SOTHERN** (1859–1933; son of E. A. Sothern, no. 30). In England, 1864–75. Debut, N.Y., 1879. With McCullough, 1880/1 and 1883. After 1887, his rich career falls into three main periods: (1) genteel British light comedy for Daniel Frohman (e.g., *The Highest Bidder*, 1887; *Lord Chumley*, 1888); (2) from 1894, swashbuckling melodrama (*The Prisoner of Zenda*, 1895; *Enemy to the King*, 1896); (3) from 1899, thoughtful, poetic drama and especially Shakespeare (*The Sunken Bell*, 1899; *Hamlet*, 1900; etc.). From 1904, teamed with Julia Marlowe (they married, 1911), appearing with her up to her retirement in 1924 (they opened the New Theatre in N.Y., 1909, with *Antony and Cleopatra*). His last N.Y. play, 1926. **88. JULIA MARLOWE** (real name, Sarah Frances Frost; 1866–1950; born in England). To U.S. as small child. At 13, in a juvenile *H.M.S. Pinafore* company in Indiana. Stardom, 1887, in romantic plays of the Mary Anderson type. Failure in N.Y., 1888; accepted there, 1896. By the turn of the century, in fewer "classic roles," but recognized as excellent in Shakespeare. In *Barbara Frietchie* (1899) and *When Knighthood Was in Flower* (1901). With Sothern, from 1904 to 1924 (see no. 87), tirelessly brought first-class Shakespeare to every corner of the nation.

89

89. **CLARA BLOODGOOD** (née Stephens; 1870–1907). Debut, 1898, at the Empire Theatre, N.Y. In the following major plays by Fitch and by Shaw: *The Climbers* (1900); *The Girl with the Green Eyes* (1902); *How He Lied to Her Husband* (1904); *Man and Superman* (1905; role in photo); *The Truth* (1907). **90. EDITH WYNNE MATTHISON** (English; 1875–1955; wife of playwright Charles Rann Kennedy). Member of a prominent family of actors, she began at age 10, making her real debut in 1896; London, 1899. U.S. debut, N.Y., 1902, in *Everyman*. With Irving in England, 1904/5. Brought back to U.S. by Henry Miller, 1908. At the New Theatre in N.Y., 1910/11 (*The Piper; The Arrow Maker;* and *The Blue Bird*); at the Little Theatre there, 1912. In 1916, she appeared with Sir Herbert Tree in *Henry VIII* in N.Y., and in *The Merry Wives of Windsor* in Boston. In 1930, she toured the U.S. in the title role of *Hamlet*. **91. AMELIA BING-HAM** (née Smiley: 1869–1927). First in N.Y. (not absolute debut), 1892, in melodrama. After many supporting roles, stardom in 1900, the year of her great success in Clyde Fitch's *The Climbers*. By 1905, however, back in stock in N.Y., and, 1908/9, in vaudeville. In *The New Henrietta* (1913; with W. H. Crane and Douglas Fairbanks). Occasional N.Y. appearances to 1926.

91

90

92

93

94

92. MARY MANNERING (real name, under which she acted in England, Florence Friend; 1876–1953; born in England; married, 1897–1910, to J. K. Hackett, no. 57). Debut in England, ca. 1890. Invited to U.S. by Daniel Frohman, 1896, as leading lady of Lyceum, N.Y.; first U.S. Trelawny in *Trelawny of the "Wells"* (1898). Star, 1900, in *Janice Meredith.* In *The Walls of Jericho* (1905) with her husband. Last N.Y. play: *The Garden of Allah* (1911). **93. VIOLA ALLEN** (1867–1948). Daughter of prominent actors, she made her debut in N.Y., 1882, succeeding Annie Russell in *Esmeralda.* McCullough's last leading lady, 1884; later with Barrett and Salvini. Leading lady of Boston Museum, 1888 (first U.S. Mrs. Errol in *Little Lord Fauntleroy*; in original production of *Shenandoah*). From 1893 to 1898, leading lady of Empire Theatre, N.Y. (first U.S. Gwendolyn in *The Importance of Being Earnest*, 1895). Star, 1898, in *The Christian.* Later successes included *The Eternal City* (1902) and *The White Sister* (1909). Among her Shakespearean performances was Lady Macbeth, on tour with J. K. Hackett, 1915/6 (N.Y., 1916). Last N.Y. play, 1918. **94. FREDERIC DE BELLEVILLE** (1850–1923; born in Belgium). Debut in London suburbs, 1873. U.S. debut, 1880, at Union Square Theatre, N.Y. Long, solid career as leading man for Clara Morris, Rose Coghlan, Mrs. Fiske and Viola Allen. Active to the year of his death.

95

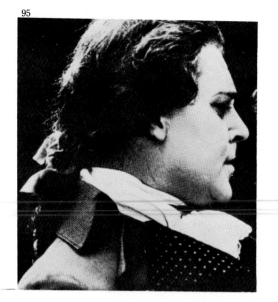

96

97

98

95/96 & 97/98. Two brothers and two sisters of the stage; both pairs from theatrical families. **95. WILLIAM FARNUM** (1876–1953). Debut in Richmond, ca. 1890; N.Y., 1890. Toured with Olga Nethersole and Viola Allen (in *The White Sister* with the latter, 1909). In *The Littlest Rebel*, with his brother and Mary Miles Minter (1911). Important film career, 1915–25. Back on N.Y. stage, 1925–29. In 1934, in Max Reinhardt's *Midsummer Night's Dream* at the Hollywood Bowl. **96. DUSTIN FARNUM** (1874–1929). Debut, 1897, in repertory; N.Y., 1899. Plays included: *Arizona* (1900); *The Virginian* (1903–07; N.Y., 1904); *Cameo Kirby* (1909); and *The Littlest Rebel* (1911). Much film work. **97. EDITH TALIAFERRO** (1893–1958). Debut (Chicago, then N.Y.), 1896, with Herne in *Shore Acres*. Many tours at turn of century, including some with Olga Nethersole and E. H. Sothern. Role of lifetime: *Rebecca of Sunnybrook Farm* (1910). In 1931, she joined the N.Y. cast of *Private Lives* and toured with the play in 1932. Last N.Y. appearance, 1935. **98. MABEL TALIAFERRO** (real given names, Maybelle Evelyn; 1887–1979). Debut, 1889, in Washington, D.C. Much child acting, with Herne and in *Children of the Ghetto* (1899). Original Lovey Mary in *Mrs. Wiggs of the Cabbage Patch* (1904). In *You Never Can Tell*, with Arnold Daly (1904). Enormous hit in *Polly of the Circus* (1907). Away from the stage in the 1920s, and rarely in N.Y. in the 1930s, she returned there in 1940 in *George Washington Slept Here*, and in 1944 in the musical *Bloomer Girl*. Active to 1951. **99. WILLIAM FAVERSHAM** (actually, Jones; 1868–1940; born in England). Debut, 1885, London; to U.S., 1887, engaged by Daniel Frohman for the Lyceum in N.Y. Joined the company at the Empire, 1893 (first U.S. Algernon in *The Importance of Being Earnest*, 1895); became a matinee idol as the leading man there, 1896–1901. In 1899, Romeo to Maude Adams' Juliet. Star, 1901. Biggest success: *The Squaw Man* (1905; also in 1921 revival). Then, actor/manager (*The Faun*, 1911; Shakespearean tours, 1913 ff.). Last N.Y. appearance, 1931, with the Chicago Civic Shakespeare Society. Last role (a contrast to the elegance of his youth): Jeeter Lester in a touring company of *Tobacco Road*, 1934. **100. GRACE GEORGE** (1879–1961; wife of major producer William Brady from 1899 to 1950, and stepmother of Alice Brady, no. 239). Performed, 1893, in graduating class of the American Academy of Dramatic Art in N.Y. Real debut, N.Y., 1894. No important roles until 1898; stardom, 1899; genuine success from 1900. In her vast and varied career, she tried all kinds of worthwhile plays, appearing in many revivals of old and newer standards. In 1915, she was the first Major Barbara in the U.S., doing the play with her own distinguished repertory company. A great hit of her later years was *Kind Lady* (1935; she was also in the 1940 revival). Also in N.Y., she did *Spring Again* in 1941, and *The Velvet Glove* in 1949. Her last appearance there was with Katharine Cornell in 1951.

101. HELEN WARE (real surname, Remer; 1877–1939). Debut as an extra with Maude Adams, N.Y., 1899. In *Under Two Flags* (1901/2), understudy to Blanche Bates; fired after playing the role of Cigarette for a week. Worked with Blanche Walsh, Otis Skinner, Minnie Dupree, Arnold Daly and others. In *The Third Degree* (1909) as star. Solid career in standard current plays. Last stage work, including N.Y., 1928. **102. ANNIE RUSSELL** (1864–1936; born in England). Dubbed the "Duse of the English-speaking stage," she was a quiet and tender actress. Debut in Montreal with Rose Eytinge, 1872 (she had come to Canada as a small child). N.Y., 1879, in a juvenile *Pinafore* company. First big role in *Esmeralda* (1881) at the Madison Square. Severe illness, 1890–94. Nat Goodwin's leading lady, 1895/6. In: *A Royal Family* (1900); *The Girl and the Judge* (1901). Pinnacle: creation of Major Barbara, London, 1905. Ran her own Old English Comedy Company, 1912 (last time in N.Y.). Last regular appearance, 1918; one performance in Florida, 1932. **103. MAXINE ELLIOTT** (real name, Jessie C. Dermot; 1868–1940). Renowned more for great beauty and presence than for her skill, she nevertheless enjoyed a successful career, having a N.Y. theater named for her in 1908. Debut before 1890. Toured U.S. with popular English actor E. S. Willard, 1890 ff. Stints with Julia Arthur, Rose Coghlan and Augustin Daly (1895) before teaming up with Nat Goodwin in 1896 (they were married, 1898–1908); with him in *Nathan Hale* (1898), *The Cowboy and the Lady* (1899), etc. Solo stardom under Charles Dillingham's management, 1903; in the two Clyde Fitch plays *Her Own Way* (1903) and *Her Great Match* (1905). Last N.Y. play, 1920; then, comfortable retirement on Riviera. Her actress sister Gertrude married the English star Sir Johnston Forbes-Robertson.

A trio of actresses associated with old-lady roles. **104. MAY ROBSON** (real surname, Robison; 1865–1942; born in Australia). This eccentric comedienne made her debut in Brooklyn, 1883; N.Y., 1886. She belonged successively to the most prestigious N.Y. stock companies: Madison Square, Union Square, Lyceum (1890–92), Palmer's (ex-Wallack's; 1893), Empire (1893–96 and at some later times; first U.S. Miss Prism in *The Importance of Being Earnest*, 1895). In: *Are You a Mason?* (1901); *Dorothy Vernon of Haddon Hall* (1903); *It Happened in Nordland* (Victor Herbert musical; 1904). Stardom, 1907, in her biggest hit, *The Rejuvenation of Aunt Mary*. Last N.Y. play, 1926. On stage in Los Angeles (she was long in the film colony) to at least 1935. **105. LOUISE CLOSSER HALE** (1872–1933). As Louise Closser: in N.Y. drama-school performance, 1894; in *Arizona* (1900) and as Prossy in the first U.S. *Candida* (1903). With the Hale added, from 1906. Major plays: *The Blue Bird* (1910); *Beyond the Horizon* and *Miss Lulu Bett* (both 1920); the Theatre Guild's 1923 revival of *Peer Gynt; Expressing Willie* (1924); Cole Porter's *Paris* (1928; her last N.Y. show). **106. EMMA DUNN** (1875–1966; born in England). First N.Y., 1907, in Mansfield's *Peer Gynt*. Later in: *The Warrens of Virginia* (1907); *The Easiest Way* (1909); *Mother* (1910; she became a universal mother figure); *Old Lady 31* (1916). Last N.Y. play, 1927. With her in the scene from *Sinners* (1915) is: **ROBERT EDESON** (1868–1931). Son of an actor, he made his debut in Brooklyn, 1887; N.Y., 1890. From 1894 to 1897 at the Empire. Success in title role of *The Little Minister* (1897). In the Chicago creation of *Arizona* (1899). Worked with Henrietta Crosman and Amelia Bingham (in *The Climbers* with her, 1900) before attaining stardom in 1902. Last N.Y. play, 1920.

107

108

109

107. JOHN (B.) MASON (1857–1919). Debut, 1878, Philadelphia. At the Boston Museum, eventually as lead, 1879–86. In *The Christian*, N.Y., 1898. As leading man at Lyceum, N.Y., 1899–1901, shone in genteel modern comedy. Afterwards with Annie Russell and Mrs. Fiske. Important later plays: *The Witching Hour* (1907); *As a Man Thinks* (1911); *The Yellow Ticket* (1914); *Common Clay* (1915). Last N.Y. play, 1917. **108. TYRONE POWER** (1869–1931; born in England; grandson of great Irish comedian of that name; father of the dashing film star). Sent to Florida to study orange raising, he started acting there in 1884. N.Y., 1891, at the Union Square. At Daly's, 1894, in *The Taming of the Shrew*. With Mrs. Fiske, 1899–1902. Other big plays: *Ulysses* (1903); *Adrea* (1905); *The Servant in the House* (1908); *Chu Chin Chow* (exotic musical; 1917); Claudius in John Barrymore's *Hamlet* (1922). Last N.Y. appearance, 1931, in *The Merchant of Venice* with the Chicago Civic Shakespeare Society. **109. THEODORE ROBERTS** (1861–1928). Best remembered for his film work with Cecil B. DeMille and others, he had a sturdy stage career behind him, having made his debut in San Francisco stock in 1894. N.Y. stage highlights: *Gismonda* (1894; with Fanny Davenport); *Arizona* (1900); *The Squaw Man* (1905); *The Bird of Paradise* (1912; with Laurette Taylor; his last in N.Y.).

110

111

112

110. MARGARET DALE (ca. 1876–1972). Long, distinguished career as lead and support, with a large proportion of hits. Debut, 1897, Philadelphia, through the good offices of Henry Miller; in N.Y., 1898. With Miller in *The Only Way* (1899); at the Empire, 1900 ff. Later plays included: *Disraeli* (1911); *Oh! Lady! Lady!* (Kern musical; 1918); *The Cradle Snatchers* (1925); *Dinner at Eight* (1932); *The Old Maid* (1935); *Tovarich* (1936); *Lady in the Dark* (Weill musical; 1941); and *The Late George Apley* (1944). Last N.Y. play, 1948. **111. CHARLOTTE WALKER** (1878–1958). Debut, 1893; with Mansfield, N.Y., 1895; with Herne, 1901. Leading lady for Hackett, 1901–05. Great success in *The Warrens of Virginia* (1907) and *The Trail of the Lonesome Pine* (1911; N.Y., 1912). Steady N.Y. career ended 1934, in *A Sleeping Clergyman*, for the Theatre Guild. Still active elsewhere, 1936. **112. JULIA DEAN** (1878–1952; niece of the very popular actress Julia Dean Hayne). Debut, 1895. Toured with Jefferson, 1897. N.Y., 1902. Worked with Goodwin, Eleanor Robson (in *Merely Mary Ann*, 1903), Bellew and Lackaye. Biggest hit: *Bought and Paid For* (1911). Last N.Y. play, 1917; retired, 1920.

113

115

114

113. HENRY WOODRUFF (1869–1916). Debut in juvenile *Pinafore* company, 1879. Child actor with Bandmann, Booth, Neilson. At the Madison Square, N.Y., 1887–91. Left stage to attend Harvard, 1894–98. Then, worked for Goodwin, Crosman, Mrs. Fiske, Bingham, Henry Miller. Stardom, 1906, in *Brown of Harvard*. In 1909 Chicago musical *The Prince of To-night*. Touring, 1910. **114. CHARLES J. RICHMAN** (1870–1940). After amateur work in his native Chicago, he joined a traveling melodrama company in 1890. N.Y., 1894, with Herne. In 1895, succeeded Maurice Barrymore as leading man of the Stockwell company in San Francisco. Leading man at Daly's, N.Y., 1896–99; later, at Lyceum (1899) and Empire (1900). With Ada Rehan, 1904. Major subsequent plays in N.Y.: *The Rose of the Rancho* (1906); *Bought and Paid For* (1911); *Strictly Dishonorable* (1930); *Biography* (1932; for the Theatre Guild). Last N.Y. play, 1936. **115. WALLACE EDDINGER** (1881–1929). Child of actors, began at tender age; N.Y., 1888. Off the stage, 1892–1902, then acted with Robert Edeson and Arthur Byron. Important later plays: *Officer 666* (1912); *Seven Keys to Baldpate* (1913); *Boomerang* (1915); *On Approval* (1926); *And So to Bed* (1927; his last in N.Y.).

Popular turn-of-the-century leading men. **116. CHARLES CHERRY** (1872–1931; born in England). Debut, 1897, London; U.S. (N.Y.), 1899. With Maxine Elliott in her two plays by Clyde Fitch, *Her Own Way* (1903) and *Her Great Match* (1905). Star, 1909. In the U.S. premieres of Shaw's *Getting Married* (1916) and of Milne's *The Dover Road* (1921). Last N.Y. play, 1923. **117.** Harold **KYRLE BELLEW** (English; 1855–1911; son of the flamboyant preacher J.C.M. Bellew). Debut, 1874, in Australia; English provinces and London, 1875. At the Haymarket and with Irving and others before U.S. debut at Wallack's in N.Y., 1885; two years at that house. From 1887 to 1898, famous acting partnership with Cora Urquhart Potter (Mrs. Brown Potter, a former society amateur). Back in Australia, 1899–1901. Solo star in U.S. from 1901. In: *A Gentleman of France* (1901; N.Y., 1902), *Raffles, the Amateur Cracksman* (1903); *The Thief* (1907; his last in N.Y.). **118. CYRIL SCOTT** (1866–1945; born in Ireland). Debut, 1883, in Paterson, N.J. Worked with Minnie Maddern (later Mrs. Fiske), Mansfield and Lotta, and at the Madison Square and Empire. In two Belasco plays, *The Girl I Left Behind Me* (1893) and *The Heart of Maryland* (1895). In several musicals: with De Wolf Hopper (1894); at Daly's (1897/8); and especially in *Florodora* (1900). Great success in *The Prince Chap*, which he played from 1905 to 1908. Long career also included: *The Lottery Man* (1909); *Polly with a Past* (1917); and *Paths of Glory* (1935). Last N.Y. play, 1936.

119. BLANCHE WALSH (1873–1915). Public appearances from 1887; N.Y., 1889. Worked for Charles Frohman and Nat Goodwin before taking over the late Fanny Davenport's emotional Sardou roles with the Davenport company, 1898–1900. Independent stardom, 1900. Active in legit and vaudeville to the very end. **120. MARIE DORO** (real name, Marie Kathryn Stewart; 1882–1956). Debut, 1901, in St. Paul. N.Y. debut, 1902, in a musical. In 1904, in Barrie plays for Charles Frohman, and in *Granny* (last play of Mrs. G. H. Gilbert). Worked with Gillette, 1905/6. Star, 1907. Most interesting part: title role of *Oliver Twist* (1912; filmed, 1916). Last N.Y. play, 1921; retired, 1922. **121. MINNIE DUPREE** (1873–1947). Acted 1886 with Tony Hart (former partner of Ned Harrigan). N.Y., 1888. A girlish, whimsical actress, she appeared in *'Way Down East* (1898); *The Climbers* (1900); and *The Music Master* (1904). Her biggest hit was *The Road to Yesterday* (1906). Later highlights of her 60-year career: *The Old Soak* (1922); *The Shame Woman* (1923); the U.S. premiere of *Outward Bound* (1924); *Dark Eyes* (1943). Last N.Y. play, 1946.

120

121

122

123

124

122. ERNEST LAWFORD (ca. 1870–1940; born in England). London debut, 1890. To U.S., 1903, engaged by Arnold Daly: in *Candida*, N.Y., that year. From 1904, over 10 years with Charles Frohman: the first U.S. Mr. Darling/Captain Hook in *Peter Pan* (1905). In 1915, the first U.S. Cusins in *Major Barbara*. Later successes: *Why Marry?* (1917; first Pulitzer Prize play); *The Circle* (1921); Polonius in Basil Sydney's modern-dress *Hamlet* (1925); *Wings Over Europe* (1928); *The Late Christopher Bean* (1932); *Mary of Scotland* (1933); *Tovarich* (1936); and *The Fabulous Invalid* (1938). Last N.Y. play, 1939.   **123. WILLIAM T. HODGE** (1874–1932). On stage from boyhood; N.Y. by 1897. In *Mrs. Wiggs of the Cabbage Patch* (1904) and Victor Herbert's *Dream City* (1906). Enormous success as an up-to-date Yankee comedian in *The Man from Home* (1908). Last N.Y. play, 1930 (with it in Chicago, 1931).   **124. HOLBROOK BLINN** (1872–1928). Son of an actress; on stage, 1878. Adult debut with a Western traveling company, early 1890s. Came East with Phoebe Davies in *The New South* (N.Y., 1892). Took company of his own to Alaska during Klondike gold rush. In N.Y., 1897, in *The Cat and the Cherub*; then, chiefly in England to 1905. Back in U.S., acted with Eleanor Robson, Arnold Daly and Mrs. Fiske (outstanding in her *Salvation Nell*, 1908). Star, 1911, in *The Boss*. In *The Bad Man* (1920) and *The Play's the Thing* (1927; his last).

125

126

Three dramatic stars who began in musical comedy. **125. ELSIE FERGUSON** (1883–1961). Debut, 1900, in a musical-comedy chorus; in musicals to 1906, including Victor Herbert's *Miss Dolly Dollars* (1905). With Bellew and Lackaye before her stardom, 1909, in *Such a Little Queen*. Acted Portia with Sir Herbert Tree in N.Y., 1916. Famous in films, 1917–20 and 1922/3. Last N.Y. stage work in *Outrageous Fortune* (1943). **126. PAULINE FREDERICK** (née Libby; 1883–1938). Sang ballads at the Boston Music Hall before going on stage in N.Y. musical comedies in 1902. In 1904/5, moved from secondary role to lead in Herbert's *It Happened in Nordland*. Began nonmusical career in 1905 with J. K. Hackett; with Charles Frohman from 1908 (in *Samson*, that year). Exclusively in films, 1915–23; more from 1927, along with her resumed stage work. Last N.Y. play: Max-well Anderson's *The Masque of Kings* (1937). Did a play in San Francisco, 1938. **127. INA CLAIRE** (née Fagan; born 1892). In vaudeville, with songs and imitations, 1907 (N.Y., 1909). In the musicals: *Jumping Jupiter* (1911; also in cast: Jeanne Eagels and Helen Broderick); *The Quaker Girl* (1911); *The Honeymoon Express* (1913); *The Girl from Utah* (original London production, 1913); and the *Ziegfeld Follies* of 1915 and 1916. First straight role: *Polly with a Past* (1917); continued her persona of a "good" girl who only appears to be "fast" in *The Gold-Diggers* (1919). Hits of the 1920s: *Bluebeard's Eighth Wife* (1921); *The Last of Mrs. Cheney* (1925). By the Thirties, established as leading American high comedienne. Later plays included: *Biography* (1932); *End of Summer* (1936); *The Fatal Weakness* (1946); *The Confidential Clerk* (1954; her last in N.Y.).

127

128. **HAIDÉE WRIGHT** (English; 1868–1943). Member of an important theatrical family, she made her debut in 1878; London, 1887. In *The Sign of the Cross* there, 1896. First toured U.S., 1909–11, in *The Passing of the Third Floor Back*. Again in N.Y. in 1913–15, 1923 (in *Will Shakespeare*), 1926, 1927/8 (as the thespian matriarch in Ferber and Kaufman's *The Royal Family*) and 1930/1. Still active, 1935. **129. DORIS KEANE** (1881–1945; married in early 1920s to Basil Sydney, no. 204). Debut in N.Y., 1903. In *The Affairs of Anatol* (1912). Stardom, 1913, in her spectacular success *Romance* (it ran to 1915 in N.Y., 1915–18 in London, and she revived it up to 1927). In O'Neill's *Welded* (1924). Last N.Y. play, 1925. Last play, 1929, in Los Angeles. **130. LENORE ULRIC(H)** (1892–1970; married in the 1930s to Sidney Blackmer, no. 278). Acted in Wisconsin before 1910; much work in Midwest before N.Y. debut in 1915. Years as a Belasco star included: *The Heart of Wetona* (1916); *Tiger Rose* (1917); *The Son-Daughter* (1919; role in photo); *Kiki* (1921); and *Lulu Belle* (1926). In *Pagan Lady* (1930). Afterwards, more seldom in N.Y. Played Charmian in Katharine Cornell's *Antony and Cleopatra*, N.Y., 1947. Active to 1954.

131. **ALLA NAZIMOVA** (real surname, Leventon; 1879–1945; born in Russia). In her native land, acted in the provinces before obtaining leads in St. Petersburg, 1904. Became leading lady with Pavel Orleneff and with him first visited London and N.Y., 1905. Urged to remain in N.Y., she first acted in English (Ibsen and other high-class plays) in 1906. N.Y. theater named for her, 1910 (the 39th Street Theatre). In *Bella Donna* (1912) and the pacifist vaudeville sketch *War Brides* (1915, at the Palace). Chiefly in films, ca. 1918–23. In N.Y., 1928, in outstanding revival of *The Cherry Orchard* at the Civic Repertory Theatre. Original Christine Mannon in *Mourning Becomes Electra* (1931). In *The Good Earth* (1932). Ibsen in N.Y., 1935 and 1936 (*Hedda Gabler* being her last play there). Did *Ghosts* in Chicago, 1937. **132. FLORENCE NASH** (née Ryan; 1888–1950). Debut in stock, 1906; N.Y., 1907. In musicals, 1908/9; in vaudeville, 1912. Two biggest N.Y. stage successes: *Within the Law* (1912) and *Merton of the Movies* (1922). Last N.Y. play, 1926 (see no. 133). **133. MARY** Honora **NASH** (née Ryan; 1885–1976; sister of the preceding; married, 1918–24, to José Ruben, no. 164). Debut, 1903, in N.Y. musical (she was in several). Highlights of long N.Y. stage career: *Alice Sit-by-the-Fire* (1905); Clyde Fitch's last play, *The City* (1909); the first U.S. Jenny Hill in *Major Barbara* (1915); *Hassan* (1924); acting team-up with sister Florence in 1925/6 (*The Two Orphans* revival, N.Y., 1926). On stage to 1932; many films, 1934 ff.

Three top comedy stars. **134. GRANT MITCHELL** (1874–1957). Debut, 1902, Chicago (in N.Y., same year) with Mansfield. Brilliant N.Y. career included: *Get-Rich-Quick Wallingford* (1910); *It Pays to Advertise* (1914); *A Tailor-Made Man* (1917); *The Hero* (1921); *Kempy* (1922); and *The Whole Town's Talking* (1923). Off the stage, 1929–37. Last N.Y. play, 1938; still active on other stages, 1948. **135. ERNEST TRUEX** (1889–1973). Debut, 1894, in Missouri. Important youthful roles in *Wildfire* (1908; with Lillian Russell; his N.Y. debut); *Rebecca of Sunnybrook Farm* (1910); and *A Good Little Devil* (1913; with Mary Pickford and Lillian Gish). Deft comedian (sometimes in musicals) in such plays as: *Very Good, Eddie* (Kern: 1915); *Six-Cylinder Love* (1921); *Whistling in the Dark* (1932); *George Washington Slept Here* (1940); and *Flahooley* (1951; musical). Member of the American Repertory Theatre, N.Y., 1946. Last N.Y. play, 1965. **136. WILLIAM COLLIER** (Sr., 1866–1944). Son of actors, on stage as child. In a juvenile *Pinafore* company, 1879. N.Y. debut, 1882, at Daly's. First adult N.Y. success: *The City Directory* (1892). Star, 1897, in *The Man from Mexico*. With Weber & Fields, 1902 and 1912. In *The Dictator* (1904). Hit of lifetime: *Nothing But the Truth* (1916). In musicals in the 1920s, including Berlin's first *Music Box Revue* (1921). Last N.Y. show, 1927; then in films.

137. DOUGLAS FAIRBANKS (Sr.; real surname, Ulman; 1883–1939). Before his fabulous career as one of the emperors of Hollywood, he was the foremost juvenile on the N.Y. stage, already indulging in the devil-may-care acrobatics of his film days. Debut, 1900, Richmond; N.Y., 1902. In 1905, in *Fantana*, his only stage musical. Popularity, 1906, in *The Man of the Hour*. Stardom, 1908. Other plays: *Officer 666* and *Hawthorne of the U.S.A.* (both 1912); *The New Henrietta* (1913); *He Came Up Smiling* and *The Show Shop* (both 1914). Films from 1915, after final tour. **138. CONWAY TEARLE** (1878–1938). Member of important acting family with branches in U.S. and England; stepbrother of eminent English star Godfrey Tearle. Though born in N.Y., he made his debut in London, 1901. With Ellen Terry in *The Vikings* (1903). N.Y., 1905; acted with Grace George, Viola Allen and Kyrle Bellew. In: *Cameo Kirby* (1909) and *Mid-Channel* (1910; with Ethel Barrymore). First U.S. Bill Walker in *Major Barbara* (1915). In interesting revivals for many years. Created the role of the drunken has-been actor in *Dinner at Eight* (1932). Last N.Y. appearance: 5 performances as Antony to Tallulah's Cleopatra, 1937. **139. EDGAR SELWYN** (1875–1944). Also a playwright; remembered especially as a manager. Debut, 1896; N.Y., 1899. In *Arizona* (1900) and *The Arab* (1911; Los Angeles, then N.Y.). Vice president and director of the Goldwyn Pictures Corporation, 1917 (the "-wyn" was borrowed by Sam Goldfish from Selwyn's name). President of the playbroking and producing firm Selwyn and Co. (continued producing even after this was dissolved in 1924).

137

138

139

140. PEDRO DE CORDOBA (1881–1950). In E. H. Sothern's company, 1902–07 (debut, 1902, Utica; 1903, N.Y.). With New Theatre in N.Y., 1909–11. Shakespeare on tour and in N.Y., with Faversham and Anglin, 1913/4. In: *Tiger Rose* (1917); Cornell's first *Candida* (1924); *See Naples and Die* (1929). Last N.Y. play, 1934. In Los Angeles area, 1941/2 season. **141.** Charles **ROLLO PETERS** (1892–1967; born in France). Also a director and designer (was portrait painter before his theatrical work). Actor and designer for the Provincetown Players, 1917, and the Washington Square Players, 1917/8 (also directed for them). The latter group developed into the Theatre Guild, with Peters as a founder; in 1919, acted in *Bonds of Interest* and *John Ferguson*. In prestigious revivals in 1920s and 1930s; Romeo for Jane Cowl, 1923. Own stock company, Detroit, 1927 (with Ann Harding). Designed the interior of the Westport Country Playhouse (a Guild offshoot) and acted there, 1931. Toured England for the USO, 1944/5. **142. WHITFORD KANE** (1881–1956; born in Ireland). Inveterate lifelong adherent of little-theater and other avant-garde groups. Debut, 1903, Belfast; London, 1910. Liverpool Repertory Theatre, 1911. N.Y., 1912; Fine Arts Theatre, Chicago, 1913; Washington Square Players, 1917. First gravedigger in John Barrymore's *Hamlet* (1922). Connected with Neighborhood Playhouse (N.Y.), Greenwich Village Theatre, Chicago Civic Shakespeare Society. In: *Elizabeth the Queen* (1930); *Yellow Jack* (1934); Maurice Evans' *Richard II* (1937) and *Hamlet* (1938); Mercury Theatre's *The Shoemaker's Holiday* (1938); *The Moon Is Down* (1942); O'Casey's *Red Roses for Me* (1955; his last in N.Y.).

143

144

145

143. Katherine **CHRYSTAL HERNE** (1883–1950; daughter of James A. Herne, no. 60). Debut, 1899, with father; N.Y., 1900, with him. With E. H. Sothern, 1902/3; Nat Goodwin, 1903–05; Arnold Daly, 1905/6. Later, in: *As a Man Thinks* (1911); *Our Betters* (1917); *Expressing Willie* (1924); and—her huge success—*Craig's Wife* (1925). Last N.Y. play, 1931. **144. CONSTANCE COLLIER** (née Hardie; 1875–1955; born in England). Daughter of actors; on stage at 3. London debut, 1893, in comic-opera chorus. Many musicals in 1890s. Leading lady for Herbert Tree, 1901–07. N.Y. debut, 1908, in *Samson*, with Gillette. Shuttled between London and N.Y. in many elegant roles. John Barrymore's London Gertrude, 1925. First Carlotta Vance in *Dinner at Eight* (N.Y., 1932). Last N.Y. play, 1939; active elsewhere, 1941. Much Hollywood acting and coaching. **145. MARGARET WYCHERLY** (née De Wolfe; 1881–1956; born in England of American parents). Debut, 1898. Much stock and touring work in Shaw, Yeats, classics. N.Y. plays included: *The Blue Bird* (1910); *Damaged Goods* (1913); *The Thirteenth Chair* (1916); *Jane Clegg* (1920); *Back to Methuselah* (world premiere, 1922); *Six Characters in Search of an Author* (1922); *The Adding Machine* (1923); and *Tobacco Road* (1933). Last N.Y. play, 1947.

146. GEORGE ARLISS (real name, Augustus George Andrews; 1868–1946; born in England). Debut, London suburbs, 1886; West End, 1890. Joining Mrs. Patrick Campbell's company in 1900, he traveled to the U.S. with her in 1901 (N.Y., 1902), then stayed on to work for Belasco in *The Darling of the Gods* (1902). For a few years, with Mrs. Fiske. Later, famous in biographical roles: *Disraeli* (1911); *Paganini* (1915); *Hamilton* (1917). Enormous hit in *The Green Goddess* (1921; triumphal return to London, 1923). In Galsworthy's *Old English* (N.Y., 1924). Last N.Y. play, 1928; last stage work, 1929. Films, 1920–37. **147. FRANK BACON** (1864–1922). Renewing a 19th-century phenomenon, he became lastingly famous for a single role. Went on stage in the West at about 25; long a San Francisco fixture. In N.Y. did only: *The Miracle Man* (1914); *The Cinderella Man* (1916); and the long-run record-breaker *Lightnin'* (1918; 1,291 performances; he was part author). **148. AUGUSTIN DUNCAN** (1873–1954; brother of famous dancer Isadora Duncan). Also a director. Debut in stock in his native San Francisco, 1893. Toured 7 years before 1900 N.Y. debut in Mansfield's *Henry V*. With Charles Coburn's open-air company, 1908–10. In the Theatre Guild's first success, *John Ferguson* (1919). Other N.Y. acting stints: *Detour* (1921); *Hell-Bent fer Heaven* (1924; role in photo); *Juno and the Paycock* (1926); Maurice Evans' *Richard II* (1937; as John of Gaunt) and *Hamlet* (1938; as the Ghost); *Lute Song* (1946; last in N.Y.)

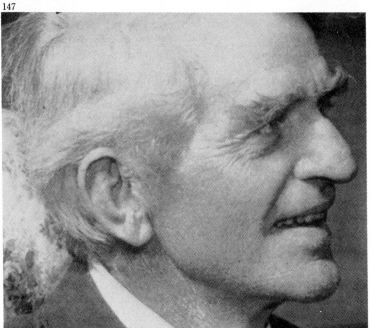

149

150

151

149. CHARLES Douville **COBURN** (1877–1961). Manager, 1894, of Savannah theater in which he had sold programs in 1891. Stock in Chicago. N.Y. (not Broadway), 1901. From 1905, manager of the Coburn Shakespearean Players. Huge N.Y. success in *The Better 'Ole* (1918). In *Bronx Express* (1922). Coburn Theatre, N.Y., 1928; did many worthy revivals. Off the stage, 1937–46 (much film work). In 1946, toured in *The Merry Wives of Windsor* for the Theatre Guild. **150. ALISON SKIPWORTH** (1863–1952; born in England). Debut, 1894, London, in the musical *A Gaiety Girl*. N.Y., 1895, in the musical *An Artist's Model*. At the Lyceum, N.Y., 1897. Shakespearean tour with Viola Allen, 1905/6. Later N.Y. plays: *The Torch-Bearers* (1922); *The Swan* (1923); and *Marseilles* (1930). Pioneer television actress, 1940. Last N.Y. play, 1942. **151. BERYL MERCER** (1882–1939; born in Spain of English parents). Debut, 1886, Yarmouth; London, 1896; N.Y., 1906. N.Y. plays included: *My Lady's Dress* (1914); *The Old Lady Shows Her Medals* (1917); *Out There* (1918); *Three Live Ghosts* (1920); *Queen Victoria* (1923; she grew gradually older during the play—long before Helen Hayes); and *Outward Bound* (1924). Last N.Y. play, 1927; then, films.

152

153

154

152. LAURA HOPE CREWS (1880–1942). On stage at 4 in San
Francisco. N.Y., 1901, in stock. In *Merely Mary Ann* (1903). With
Henry Miller, 1906 ff., including Moody's *The Faith Healer* (1909).
Highlights of long, varied stage career on both coasts: *Peter Ibbetson*
(1917) and the possessive mother in *The Silver Cord* (1926). Last
N.Y. play, 1938. In Chicago company of *Arsenic and Old Lace*,
1941. **153. PATRICIA COLLINGE** (real given names, Eileen
Cecilia; 1894–1974; born in Ireland). Debut, 1904, London; N.Y.,
1908. In: *The Blue Bird* (1910); *Everywoman* (1911); *The New
Henrietta* (1913; first of several plays, through 1915, with Douglas
Fairbanks). Big hit in *Pollyanna* (Chicago, 1915; N.Y., 1916; tours to
1918). Important revivals in 1920s. Later, in *Autumn Crocus* (1932);
The Little Foxes (1939); *Arsenic and Old Lace*, 1941 (succeeding
Josephine Hull); *The Heiress* (1947). Last N.Y. play, 1952. In U.S.
premiere of *Live Like Pigs*, Boston, 1965. **154. ROSE STAHL**
(1870–1955; born in Canada). Debut, 1897, Philadelphia; N.Y., same
year. Star, 1902. She developed her 1904 vaudeville sketch *The Chorus Lady* into a full-length play, which she did for years, beginning in
1906. Another N.Y. success: *Maggie Pepper* (1911). Last N.Y. play,
1916; retired, 1918.

155

156

157

155. BILLIE BURKE (real given names, Ethelbert Appleton; 1884–1970; married to Florenz Ziegfeld, 1914–32). Daughter of a clown, she toured in Europe, 1898/9, and played a first-rate London music hall in 1902. In London musicals, 1903–07. Brought to N.Y. by Charles Frohman, 1907, as leading lady for John Drew. Star, 1908; in: *Mrs. Dot* (1910); *The "Mind-the-Paint" Girl* (1912). Continued in light society plays in N.Y. to 1930. Did plays in the Los Angeles area, 1931–34. Back in N.Y., 1943/4. Active on stage elsewhere to 1958.   **156. JANET BEECHER** (1884–1955). Debut, 1904, N.Y. With Nat Goodwin, 1908/9. Important N.Y. plays: *The Lottery Man* (1909); *The Concert* (1910); *The Great Adventure* (1913); *Fair and Warmer* (1915); *A Bill of Divorcement* (1921). Lapse after 1932. Back in 1944 in last N.Y. play, *The Late George Apley* (also in Chicago, 1946).   **157. EMILY STEVENS** (1882–1928; younger cousin of Mrs. Fiske, no. 72). In N.Y., 1901, with her aunt; with her 6 more years. In 1908, in *The Devil*, with George Arliss (produced by *Mr.* Fiske); gained attention touring with Arliss in *Septimus*, 1909. Later plays on her own: *The Boss* (1911); the Chicago premiere of *Within the Law* (1912); *The Unchastened Woman* (1915; her biggest hit, played 3 years); and *Fata Morgana* (1924). Last N.Y. play, 1925.

159

158

160

158. MARGARET ILLINGTON (née Maud Light; 1881–1934; married to Daniel Frohman, later to Major Edward Bowes). Debut, 1900, with J. K. Hackett, for Daniel Frohman. At the Lyceum and Daly's; with Sothern, 1902/3. Opposite Drew in *His House in Order* (1906) and Bellew in *The Thief* (1907). In *The Lie* (1914). Last N.Y. play, 1919. **159. JANE COWL** (1884–1950). Debut, 1903, N.Y., in small part for Belasco; continued filling small roles in his plays: *The Music Man* (1904); *The Rose of the Rancho* (1906); *A Grand Army Man* (1907); and *The Easiest Way* (1909); better parts from 1909. First big hit: *Within the Law* (1912). In: *Common Clay* (1915); *Lilac Time* (1917; part author); *Smilin' Through* (1919; part author); a sensational *Romeo and Juliet* (1923; 157 consecutive performances); *The Road to Rome* (1927); *Rain from Heaven* (1934); and her last play, *First Lady* (N.Y., 1935/6; Chicago, 1936/7). **160. MARJORIE RAMBEAU** (ca. 1889–1970). Stage debut, 1901, in San Francisco (earlier, had sung in Alaska); much West Coast stock. N.Y. 1913. In: *Cheating Cheaters* (1916); *Eyes of Youth* (1917); and many other popular N.Y. successes to 1926. Later, in more West Coast stock; in San Francisco, 1938. Much film work.

161. ROBERT LORAINE (English; 1876–1935). Debut, 1889, in the English provinces; London, 1896. Served in Boer War. U.S. debut, N.Y., 1901. Toured with Grace George. First U.S. John Tanner in *Man and Superman* (1905). Fame as R.A.F. air ace in World War I. Back on London stage, 1919. Further N.Y. appearances in 1924, 1926, 1930 (*Canaries Sometimes Sing*) and 1935. **162. LEO** James **DITRICH-STEIN** (also Dietrichstein; 1865–1928; born in Hungary). Charming and magnetic romantic actor, at ease in comedy. Debut in Vienna; to U.S., 1890, acting in German at the Irving Place Theatre, N.Y. Soon began acting in English. In: the original *Trilby* (1895); *Are You a Mason?* (1901); *The Concert* (1910); *The Great Lover* (1915; he was author); and *The King* (1917). Last N.Y. play, 1922; on stage in Chicago, 1924. **163. WALTER HAMPDEN** (actually, Walter Hampden Dougherty; 1879–1955). Debut, 1901, England, with F. R. Benson; stayed in that Shakespearean troupe to 1904, year of London debut. Exponent of poetic drama. U.S. debut, N.Y., 1907; in *The Servant in the House* (1907; N.Y., 1908); hired by Henry Miller to support Nazimova in N.Y., 1907. In *The City*, 1909. At the Fine Arts Theatre, Chicago, 1913. In *Good Gracious Annabelle* (N.Y., 1916). First big Shakespearean venture on his own, 1918; first played Cyrano, 1923. Hampden's Theatre, N.Y. (the Colonial), 1925–30; *Caponsacchi* (1926). Endless revivals and tours. Last play: Arthur Miller's *The Crucible* (N.Y., 1953).

164. Helen Westley and José Ruben in *Another Way Out,* 1916. **HELEN WESTLEY** (1879–1942). First N.Y. appearance, 1897. Joined Washington Square Players, N.Y., 1915, and became founder of the Theatre Guild, which developed from that group. From 1919 to 1935, acted only for the Guild, in such plays as: *Heartbreak House* (world premiere, 1920); *He Who Gets Slapped* and *R.U.R.* (both 1922); *The Adding Machine* (1923); *The Guardsman* (1924); *Strange Interlude* (1928); and *They Shall Not Die* (1934). **JOSÉ RUBEN** (1886–1969; born in France; married, 1918–24, to Mary Nash, no. 133). First acted here in French in 1909, having come to the U.S. with Sarah Bernhardt. His first English-speaking role in N.Y. was in *The Garden of Allah* (1911). Continued in flamboyant, exotic parts. With Washington Square Players, 1916/7. In Kern's *The Cat and the Fiddle* (1931); *Rain from Heaven* (1934). In 1944 ff., directed operetta in Dallas. Last N.Y. play: *The Great Sebastians,* 1956, with the Lunts.

165

166

167

165. ANN ANDREWS (born 1895). Debut, 1916, Los Angeles, and 1917, N.Y., in *Nju*. In: *The Captive* (1926); *The Royal Family* (1927); *Dinner at Eight* (1932); *Three Waltzes* (1937; last in N.Y.). Active to 1947.   **166. FAY** Okell **BAINTER** (1891–1968). Debut, 1898, in Los Angeles; sang in repertory in the West and in vaudeville in the East. N.Y. debut, 1912, in musical *The Rose of Panama*. Huge hit as Ming Toy in *East Is West* (1918; with song). In Victor Herbert's *The Dream Girl* (1924). In major revivals in late 1920s and early 1930s. In *Dodsworth* (1934; last in N.Y.). Much stage activity outside of N.Y. up to 1962 (in national company of *Long Day's Journey into Night*, 1957/8). Much film work (Oscar for *Jezebel*, 1938).   **167. MADGE KEN-NEDY** (born ca. 1890). After amateur work, professional debut in 1910 (tour with Henry Woodruff); N.Y., 1912. In: *Fair and Warmer* (1915); *Poppy* (1923; musical, with W. C. Fields); Philip Barry's *Paris Bound* (1927). Succeeded Gertrude Lawrence in *Private Lives* (N.Y., 1931). Last N.Y. play, 1932. In Chicago, 1934.

168

169

170

Three leading juveniles of the 1920s. **168. ROBERT AMES** (1889–1931; married to Vivienne Segal). In New England stock before N.Y. debut, 1916, in *Come Out of the Kitchen*, with Ruth Chatterton. Tour with Otis Skinner, ca. 1920. In the N.Y. plays *Nice People* and *The Hero* (both 1921) and *Icebound* (1923). Last N.Y. play, 1928. Films from 1925. **169. NORMAN FOSTER** (1903–1976; married to Claudette Colbert, later to Sally Blane). Reporter and film extra (1924) before going on stage in Brooklyn, 1924. In the N.Y. plays: *The Poor Nut* (1925); *The Barker* (1927; with Colbert and Walter Huston); *Night Hostess* (1928); and *June Moon* (1929). Then back to films, 1930 (eventually directed more than he acted). **170. GREGORY KELLY** (1891–1927; married to Ruth Gordon, no. 260). As a child actor, he performed with Jefferson in *Rip Van Winkle* at age 4; later, with Mrs. Fiske. In N.Y. he was in the musical *School Days* (1908) and in *Kismet* (1911; with Otis Skinner). He was long associated with Stuart Walker's Indianapolis-based Portmanteau Theatre as actor and co-director (with the troupe in N.Y., 1916); that group, befriended by Booth Tarkington, developed the play *Seventeen* in which Kelly starred with Ruth Gordon (N.Y., 1918). Later, in *Dulcy* (Chicago, then N.Y., 1921; with Lynn Fontanne) and *The Butter-and-Egg Man* (1925). Much activity in Chicago.

64

171

172

173

Three more young male leads. **171. RALPH FORBES** (1905–1951; born in England; married to Ruth Chatterton, no. 194, later to Heather Angel). Debut in England, 1922; London, 1924; N.Y., 1924. That year, in the musical *Magnolia Lady*, with Chatterton. With her in *The Man with a Load of Mischief* (1925). Hollywood films, 1926–41, then in worthwhile revivals and tours. In N.Y. with Cornell in *The Doctor's Dilemma* (1941). Last N.Y. play: revival of *Caesar and Cleopatra*, 1949. **172. EUGENE O'BRIEN** (ca. 1881–1966). Debut in N.Y. musical, 1905. In: *The Builder of Bridges* (1909; with Bellew); *The Million* (1911); and the revival of *Trelawny of the "Wells"* with Ethel Barrymore (1911). Though principally an extremely popular film star from 1915 until the advent of talkies, he appeared in several more N.Y. plays up to 1923. **173. KENNETH MacKENNA** (born 1899; real name, Leo Mielziner, Jr.; brother of designer Jo Mielziner; was married to Kay Francis). Debut, 1919, N.Y. In: *The World We Live In* (1922); Philip Barry's *You and I* (1922); and the 1926 revival of *What Every Woman Knows*, with Helen Hayes. Steady N.Y. stage work to 1937. From 1937 to 1942, scenario head for MGM, returning to that job after World War II. N.Y. play (last), 1959.

174

175

174. MARY MORRIS (1895–1970). Amateur, then understudy for Washington Square Players, N.Y., before making debut with them in *The Clod*, 1916. In stock, World War I camp shows, pageants. With the San Francisco Theatre Guild, 1922. Back in N.Y., with the Provincetown Players, 1924: that year, in *Fashion* revival and O'Neill's *Desire Under the Elms*. For Group Theatre, in *The House of Connelly* and *1931* (both 1931) and *Night Over Taos* (1932). In *Within the Gates*, 1934. Seldom on Broadway in the rest of her distinguished career; at the fine off-Broadway Phoenix Theatre, 1956; acted to at least 1961. Also a teacher and director. **175. MARY SERVOSS** (ca. 1888–1968). Debut in Chicago stock, 1905; N.Y., 1906. Classic roles in Midwest, 1911–16. First Broadway part, 1912; more steady N.Y. work from 1916. Portia to Warfield's Shylock, 1922 (role in photo). Later N.Y. highlights:

Street Scene (1929); Gertrude in Raymond Massey's *Hamlet* (1931) and in Leslie Howard's (1936); *Counsellor-at-Law* (1931; with Muni); *Dangerous Corner* (1932); *Tortilla Flat* (1938). Last N.Y. appearance in Judith Anderson's *Medea* at the City Center, 1949. **176. JEANNE EAGELS** (1890–1929). One of the most spellbinding natural talents in the history of the American theater. Debut, 1897, in Kansas City. Long, obscure history of tent shows, road companies and bit parts. In N.Y. musical *Jumping Jupiter*, 1911. With Arliss, 1917. In the N.Y. plays *Daddies* (1918), *A Young Man's Fancy* (1919), *The Wonderful Thing* (1920) and *In the Night Watch* (1921) before soaring to the heights of celebrity as Sadie Thompson in *Rain* (1922). With Leslie Howard in *Her Cardboard Lover* (1927; her last in N.Y.). A few films; she sears the screen in the 1929 movie version of *The Letter*.

177

178

179

177. ABBIE MITCHELL (ca. 1884–1960). On stage at the turn of the century. Earlier career, in musicals and plays with music (was married to composer Will Marion Cook): *The Southerners* (N.Y.; 1904); *Rufus Rastus* (Philadelphia; 1906; with Ernest Hogan); *Bandanna Land* (N.Y.; 1908); *The Red Moon* (N.Y.; 1909). Later N.Y. plays (speaking roles, with one big exception): *In Abraham's Bosom* (1926); *Coquette* (1927); *Stevedore* (1934; in its second season); Gershwin's opera *Porgy and Bess* (1935; as Clara, opening the evening with "Summertime"); *The Little Foxes* (1939; role in photo); *On Whitman Avenue* (1946; last in N.Y.) **178. CHARLES S**(idney) **GILPIN** (1878–1930). Debut, 1896, with a minstrel company. Vaudeville, jubilee singing. With (Bert) Williams & Walker, 1905. With Pekin Players, Chicago. Only 2 N.Y. roles, but one was significant and the other titanic: in Drinkwater's *Abraham Lincoln* (1919) and as the original Brutus Jones in O'Neill's *The Emperor Jones* (1920). **179. PAUL ROBESON** (1898–1976). N.Y. debut at Lafayette Theatre in Harlem, 1921. Broadway, 1922; same year, acted with Mrs. Patrick Campbell in Blackpool, England. Back in N.Y., original lead in O'Neill's *All God's Chillun Got Wings* (1924); in the 1924 and 1925 revivals of *The Emperor Jones*; London debut in that play, 1925. In *Black Boy* (N.Y., 1926); took over role of Crown in *Porgy*, 1928. Joe in first London *Show Boat* (1928) and in first N.Y. revival (1932). In musical play *John Henry* (1940; role in photo). Played Othello, 1942–45 (N.Y., 1943; 295 performances). Worldwide concertizing between 1931 and 1961. Films, U.S. and England.

180. From left to right in this scene from *Porgy* (1927): Rose McClendon as Serena, Frank Wilson as Porgy and Evelyn Ellis as Bess. **ROSE McCLENDON** (1885–1936). Other N.Y. plays included: *Deep River* (musical) and *In Abraham's Bosom* (both 1926); *The House of Connelly* (1931); and *Mulatto* (1935; fatal illness during the run). In 1935 she organized the Negro People's Theatre, which inspired the black unit of the Federal Theatre Project. **FRANK WILSON** (ca. 1886–1956). After minstrelsy and vaudeville, in Harlem plays in 1914. In original O'Neill *All God's Chillun Got Wings* (1924) and *The Dreamy Kid* (1925) and the 1925 *Emperor Jones* revival. Played two roles during run of *In Abraham's Bosom* (1926/7). Later N.Y. plays: *They Shall Not Die* (1934); *Green Pastures* (1935; as Moses); *Watch on the Rhine* (1941); *Take a Giant Step* (1953; last in N.Y.). **EVELYN ELLIS** (ca. 1894–1958). Debut, 1919, at Lafayette Theatre in Harlem. Broadway career began 1927 in revival of *Goat Alley*. Later: *Native Son* (1941); *Deep Are the Roots* (1945); the black *Tobacco Road* (1950); and the 1951 revival of *The Royal Family*. Last Broadway, 1953; some off-Broadway, 1954.

181

182

183

181. O. P. HEGGIE (1879–1936; born in Australia). Debut, 1899, in Adelaide; London, 1906. U.S. tour with Ellen Terry, 1907 (first N.Y. *Captain Brassbound's Conversion*); in U.S. again, 1912; regularly from 1914. First N.Y. Androcles in Shaw's play, 1915. In: *Justice* (1916); *The Truth About Blaydes* (1922); *Minick* (1924); a number of prestigious revivals; and *The Green Bay Tree* (1933; his last in N.Y.). **182. LOWELL** (J.) **SHERMAN** (1885–1934). On stage as child; much stock. N.Y., 1904. Pony Express rider in *The Girl of the Golden West* (1905). Acted with Mrs. Leslie Carter and Nat Goodwin. Became popular as smooth villain in melodramas and crime plays. In *The Fool* (1922). Last N.Y. play: *The Woman Disputed* (1926; toured in it, 1927). Then, films, as actor and director. **183. LOUIS** Robert **WOLHEIM** (1881–1931). Math teacher and mining engineer before actor. N.Y., 1920. His two great stage roles: Yank in O'Neill's *The Hairy Ape* (1922) and Captain Flagg in *What Price Glory* (1924; last in N.Y.). Chicago play, 1926. Significant film appearances.

184. RICHARD BENNETT (1872–1944; father of Constance, Barbara and Joan Bennett). Debut, 1891, in Chicago; N.Y., same year. Fairly steady work in N.Y. from 1897 (connection with Charles Frohman to ca. 1910). Plays included: *The Royal Family* (1900); *Man and Superman* and *The Lion and the Mouse* (both 1905); *What Every Woman Knows* (1909; opposite Maude Adams); *Damaged Goods* (1913); O'Neill's first full-length play, *Beyond the Horizon* (1920); *He Who Gets Slapped* (1922); *They Knew What They Wanted* (1924; opposite Pauline Lord); and *Winterset* (1935; his last in N.Y.).

185

186

187

Major young leading men of the 1920s. **185. ELLIOT CABOT** (1899–1938). Debut, 1922, N.Y., in *Six Characters in Search of an Author*. Later, in: *Sun-Up* (1923); *The Great Gatsby* and *The Silver Cord* (both 1926); and *Coquette* (1927). From 1928, acted regularly for the Theatre Guild. Active to about 1937. **186. EARLE LARIMORE** (1899–1947). Debut, 1906, in his native Portland, Ore. His relative, Laura Hope Crews, got him into stock with Jessie Bonstelle; he also worked with Stuart Walker. N.Y., 1925. With the Theatre Guild from 1926, his plays included: *The Silver Cord* (1926); *The Second Man* (1927); *Strange Interlude* (1928); *Hotel Universe* (1930); *Mourning Becomes Electra* (1930); *The Good Earth* (1932); and *Biography* (1932). Regular N.Y. work ended 1935; on West Coast with Eva Le Gallienne, 1939/40. In 1947, understudied in N.Y., and went on the road in *The Iceman Cometh*. **187.** Francis **MORGAN FARLEY** (born 1898). Appearance in Cleveland, 1916. Debut touring with Stuart Walker, 1916–19 (in N.Y., 1918, in *Seventeen*). In: *Deburau* (1920); *Fata Morgana* (1924); *An American Tragedy* (1926). At Civic Repertory Theatre, 1930/1. Later in 1930s (in N.Y.): *Crime and Punishment* (1935); Osric in Gielgud's *Hamlet* (1936); member of Mercury Theatre, 1937/8; *Outward Bound* revival (1938). Active on stage to 1940; in films, into the 1950s.

188

189

190

Three great women of the Theatre Guild. **188. WINIFRED LENIHAN** (1898–1964). Debut, 1918, N.Y. In *The Dover Road* (1921) and *Will Shakespeare* (1923). In 1923, for the Guild, in the title role of the world premiere of Shaw's *Saint Joan*. Later, in *White Wings* (1926) and a *Major Barbara* revival (1928; role in photo). Last N.Y. play, 1936. In 1925 founded the Guild's School of Acting. **189. MARGALO GILLMORE** (born 1897 in London). Debut, 1917; in N.Y. that year. In: *The Famous Mrs. Fair* (1919); O'Neill's *The Straw* (1921); *He Who Gets Slapped* (Guild; 1922); *Outward Bound* (1924); *The Green Hat* (1925). More Guild plays: *Juarez and Maximilian*; *Ned McCobb's Daughter*; and *The Silver Cord* (all 1926); *The Second Man* (1927); and O'Neill's *Marco Millions* (1928). Also in: *Berkeley Square* (1929); *The Women* (1936); and *No Time for Comedy* (1939). Took over many Broadway roles and acted in many London casts of U.S. plays. Last N.Y. show: *Sail Away* (1961). **190. CLARE EAMES** (1896–1930; married to playwright Sidney Howard). Debut, 1918, N.Y. In *Déclassée* (1919; with Ethel Barrymore). In 1924: in the revival of *Fashion*, and Lady Macbeth for J. K. Hackett. Guild plays included: *Lucky Sam McCarver* (1925); *Juarez and Maximilian* (1926; as Carlotta); and *Ned McCobb's Daughter* (also 1926). In London, 1927–29.

191. William **LEE TRACY** (1898–1968). In vaudeville sketches, 1919; stock and tours, 1920–24. N.Y., 1924, in *The Show-Off*. Great success in *Broadway* (1926), topped by that in *The Front Page* (1928). Off the stage, 1931–35 (in major films). In 1938, succeeded Raymond Massey in the London run of *Idiot's Delight*. Last N.Y. plays: *The Best Man* (1960) and *Minor Miracle* (1965). **192. GLENN HUNTER** (1893–1945). A splendid juvenile. Debut, N.Y., 1916, in the second season of the Washington Square Players. Later, in: *Seventeen* (1918); *Clarence* (1919); *Merton of the Movies* (1922); *Young Woodley* (1925); and the Rodgers & Hart musical *Spring Is Here* (1929). Last N.Y. play, 1938. **193. GEORGE GAUL** (1885–1939). Debut, 1909, N.Y. Toured with Billie Burke, Otis Skinner, Charles Coburn and others. N.Y. appearances with Stuart Walker in 1918 (*Seventeen*) and 1919. In the world premiere of *Back to Methuselah* for the Theatre Guild, 1922. In same year, biggest hit, as Chico in *Seventh Heaven* (role in photo). In O'Neill's *Dynamo* (1929). Last N.Y. play, 1932.

194. RUTH CHATTERTON (1893–1961; married to Ralph Forbes, no. 171, then to George Brent). Debut, 1909, Washington, D.C.; N.Y., 1911. Very popular in *Daddy Long-Legs* (1914) and *Come Out of the Kitchen* (1916). In Barrie's *Mary Rose* (1920) and the musical *Magnolia Lady* (1924). Absent from N.Y. stage (some work on West Coast and London), 1927–37. Much touring. Last N.Y. play, 1951. **195. HELEN MENKEN** (1901–1966; married for a time to Humphrey Bogart). N.Y., 1906; stock, 1911–15. N.Y. hits included: *Three Wise Fools* (1918); *Seventh Heaven* (1922; as Diane); *The Captive* (1926); *Mary of Scotland* (1933; as Queen Elizabeth); and *The Old Maid* (1935). Last Broadway play, 1936, but active to at least 1961. Producer of the Stage Door Canteen, N.Y., 1942–46. **196. JUNE WALKER** (1899–1966; mother of actor John Kerr). N.Y. debut, 1918, in a revue chorus. A talented comedienne especially, she was in: *Six-Cylinder Love* (1921); *The Nervous Wreck* (1923); *Processional* (1925); *Gentlemen Prefer Blondes* (1926; role in photo, with blonde wig for role of Lorelei Lee); *The Bachelor Father* (1928); *Green Grow the Lilacs* (1931); *The Farmer Takes a Wife* (1934); and *The Middle of the Night* (1956). In national company of *Death of a Salesman*, 1949/50. Last N.Y. play, 1958; active to at least 1961.

197. **LUCILLE LA VERNE** (1872–1945). On stage as child; N.Y., 1888, with Fanny Davenport. Much work in San Francisco; own company in Richmond. In N.Y., 1923, in: *East of Suez* and her huge hit *Sun-Up* (role in photo; run and revivals through 1929, some at her own theater). Last N.Y. play, 1936. **198. FANIA MARINOFF** (1890–1971; born in Russia; married to writer and photographer Carl Van Vechten). Debut, 1898, in Denver stock; N.Y., 1903. With Mrs. Patrick Campbell and Arnold Daly. Much Shakespeare, Ibsen, other classics. In *Tarnish* (1923). Away from stage, 1924–31. Last N.Y. play, 1937; active to at least 1948. **199. DUDLEY DIGGES** (1879–1947; born in Ireland). A founder of the Irish National Theatre in 1902, he came to the U.S. in 1904 and was regularly in N.Y. from 1908. Stage manager for Arliss 7 years (in *Disraeli*, 1911). Charter acting member of Theatre Guild, in such plays as: *Heartbreak House* (1920); *Liliom* (1921); *The Adding Machine* (1923); *The Guardsman* (1924); and *Marco Millions* (1928). Great later triumphs: *On Borrowed Time* (1938) and *The Iceman Cometh* (1946). Connected with the Equity Players and the Actors' Theatre. **200. JAMES RENNIE** (1890–1965; born in Canada; married, 1920–35, to Dorothy Gish, no. 251). Debut, 1908; regularly in N.Y. from 1919. In: *The Great Gatsby* (1926; title role); *Alien Corn* and *Murder at the Vanities* (both 1933); and *Remains to Be Seen* (1951). Last N.Y. play, 1958. **201. LAURETTE TAYLOR** (née Cooney; 1884–1946). In vaudeville as child. Play debut, 1903, Boston, then N.Y. Popular star of old-fashioned, low-price melodrama in Seattle. Back in N.Y., 1909, in a play by J. Hartley Manners, whom she married. In *Alias Jimmy Valentine* (1910) and *The Bird of Paradise* (1912) before her huge success in *Peg o' My Heart* (1912) in N.Y. and London. Later, in: *Out There* (1917); *Humoresque* (1923); and Philip Barry's *In a Garden* (1925). Away from stage, 1928–32; drinking problem; broke down during run of return play, 1932. Brilliant comeback in *Outward Bound* revival of 1938; stratospheric glory in *The Glass Menagerie* (Chicago, 1944; N.Y., 1945).

Sincerely
Laurette Taylor

MISHKIN
N.Y.

203

202

204

202. FRITZ LEIBER (1883–1949). In Chicago stock, 1902–05. Traveled with the Shakespeareans Ben Greet, 1905–07 (N.Y., 1905), Julia Marlowe (1908) and Robert Mantell (1908–15 and 1916–18). Own Shakespeare company, 1918. From 1924, N.Y. appearances in modern plays, including *The Field God* (1927). With the Chicago Civic Shakespeare Society, 1929–32 (last N.Y., 1931). Toured with own company, 1934–35; then, in films. **203. HENRY STEPHENSON** (real surname, Garraway; 1871–1956; born on Grenada, B.W.I.). Debut, 1896, provinces; London, same year. With Charles Hawtrey 8 years, including 3 U.S. trips (N.Y., 1901). In the play *An Englishman's Home* (London, 1909). Permanently in U.S. from 1909; with Mrs. Fiske and Nazimova. In *Justice* (1916). With Jane Cowl, 1916–20, including *Lilac Time* (1917) and *Smilin' Through* (1919). In *The Fool* (1922). Films, 1932–49. Last N.Y. play: *That Lady* (1949), with Katharine Cornell. **204. BASIL SYDNEY** (English; real surname, Nugent; 1894–1968; married to Doris Keane, no. 129, before marriage to Mary Ellis, 1929–36). On stage, 1909, provinces; 1913, London; Old Vic, 1914. U.S. tour with Granville-Barker, 1914, in *Fanny's First Play*. In U.S. again, 1920, with Doris Keane, staying to 1934 and appearing in: *R.U.R.* (1922); Ethel Barrymore's *Romeo and Juliet* (1922; as Mercutio); his famous modern-dress *Hamlet* (1925); and *Children of Darkness* (1930). Active in England to at least 1965. Best remembered in U.S. today as Claudius in Olivier's film of *Hamlet* (1948).

207

206

205. BASIL RATHBONE (1892–1967; born in South Africa). In Frank Benson's Shakespeare troupe, 1911–15 (U.S. trip, 1912). Important work in London, including male lead in Maugham's *East of Suez* (1922). Often in N.Y. from 1922; in *The Swan* (1923) and *The Captive* (1926). With Katharine Cornell, 1933/4; her Romeo in N.Y. (1934). Later N.Y. plays: *The Heiress* (1947); *The Gioconda Smile* (1950); *Jane* (1952); *Sherlock Holmes* (1953; unsuccessful exploitation of popular film characterization); and *J. B.* (1959; his last in N.Y.). Active on stage to 1960; then, readings and lectures. **206. OTTO KRUGER** (1885–1974). Debut, 1900, Toledo. Much stock and vaudeville before N.Y. debut, 1915. In many comedies as well as dramas: *Seven Chances* (1916); *To the Ladies* (1922); *The Nervous Wreck* (1923); *The Royal Family* (1927; as Tony Cavendish); succeeding Noël Coward in *Private Lives* in 1931 and Paul Muni in *Counsellor-at-Law* in 1932; *The Moon Is Down* (1942). Last N.Y., 1949; last play, 1952, Los Angeles. TV work from 1934 in London. **207. LIONEL ATWILL** (1885–1946; born in England). Debut, 1905, London. In the famous Gaiety company, Manchester, 1915; that year to U.S. (including N.Y.) with Lillie Langtry. Own management in N.Y., 1917/8, doing Ibsen and other fine plays. In *Deburau* (1920) and the Theatre Guild's revival of *Caesar and Cleopatra* (1925). Last stage work, including N.Y., 1931; then, films.

208

209

210

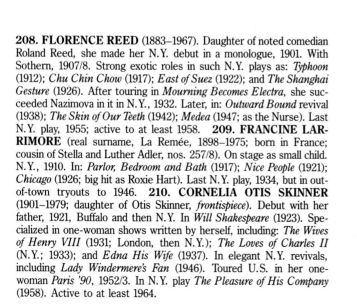

208. FLORENCE REED (1883–1967). Daughter of noted comedian Roland Reed, she made her N.Y. debut in a monologue, 1901. With Sothern, 1907/8. Strong exotic roles in such N.Y. plays as: *Typhoon* (1912); *Chu Chin Chow* (1917); *East of Suez* (1922); and *The Shanghai Gesture* (1926). After touring in *Mourning Becomes Electra*, she succeeded Nazimova in it in N.Y., 1932. Later, in: *Outward Bound* revival (1938); *The Skin of Our Teeth* (1942); *Medea* (1947; as the Nurse). Last N.Y. play, 1955; active to at least 1958.   **209. FRANCINE LAR-RIMORE** (real surname, La Remée, 1898–1975; born in France; cousin of Stella and Luther Adler, nos. 257/8). On stage as small child. N.Y., 1910. In: *Parlor, Bedroom and Bath* (1917); *Nice People* (1921); *Chicago* (1926; big hit as Roxie Hart). Last N.Y. play, 1934, but in out-of-town tryouts to 1946.   **210. CORNELIA OTIS SKINNER** (1901–1979; daughter of Otis Skinner, *frontispiece*). Debut with her father, 1921, Buffalo and then N.Y. In *Will Shakespeare* (1923). Specialized in one-woman shows written by herself, including: *The Wives of Henry VIII* (1931; London, then N.Y.); *The Loves of Charles II* (N.Y.; 1933); and *Edna His Wife* (1937). In elegant N.Y. revivals, including *Lady Windermere's Fan* (1946). Toured U.S. in her one-woman *Paris '90*, 1952/3. In N.Y. play *The Pleasure of His Company* (1958). Active to at least 1964.

211

212

213

211. EVA LE GALLIENNE (born 1899 in London; daughter of writer Richard Le Gallienne). Debut, 1914, London; N.Y., 1915. Noteworthy in *Liliom* (1921) and *The Swan* (1923). Worldwide fame as actress/manager of the Civic Repertory Theatre in N.Y., 1926–33, doing Ibsen, Chekhov, Goldoni, Tolstoy, Shakespeare, Molière and modern classics (*Alice in Wonderland*, 1932). Much touring in later 1930s. In N.Y. play *Uncle Harry*, 1942. Shortlived American Repertory Theatre in N.Y., 1946/7, with Cheryl Crawford and Margaret Webster. In N.Y. revival of *The Royal Family*, 1975. In jubilee production of *Alice in Wonderland*, N.Y., 1982. 212. PAULINE LORD (1890–1950). Glowing emotional actress. Debut, 1903, San Francisco; first in N.Y., 1905, touring with Nat Goodwin. Success in N.Y. from 1921 upon creation of *Anna Christie*. Later, in: *They Knew What They Wanted* (1924); tour of *Strange Interlude* (1928/9); *The Late Christopher Bean* (1932); and *Ethan Frome* (1936). In N.Y. to 1944. Last play: the Boston *Glass Menagerie*, 1947. 213. HOPE WILLIAMS (born 1901). After amateur work in a socially exclusive comedy club, she made her professional debut in Barry's *Paris Bound* (N.Y.; 1927), then appeared in his *Holiday* (1928) and in: *Rebound* (1930); *The New Yorkers* (1930; Porter musical); *Too True to Be Good* (1932; Theatre Guild); *Strike Me Pink* (1933); and a 1939 revival of *The Importance of Being Earnest* (as Miss Prism).

214

215

The greatest man-and-wife acting team in American stage history—"the Lunts." **214 & 216. ALFRED LUNT** (1892–1977). Debut, 1912, in Boston stock (the Castle Square Company). With Margaret Anglin and Lillie Langtry, 1914–16. N.Y., 1917. Came to critics' attention in *Clarence* (1919). First appeared in play with Lynn Fontanne, 1919, Washington D.C.; they married in 1922. He was in the first U.S. *Outward Bound* (1924) before the couple teamed up in N.Y. for the first time (that same year) in *The Guardsman*, for the Theatre Guild. Subsequent Guild plays (* = with Fontanne): *Juarez and Maximilian* and *Ned McCobb's Daughter* (both 1926); *The Second Man* (1927;*); *Marco Millions* (1928); *Elizabeth the Queen* (1930;*); *Reunion in Vienna* (1931;*); and *The Taming of the Shrew* (1935;*; see photo 216; in that year, he became a director of the Guild). From 1930 to 1960, the

Lunts always acted together; their other plays included: *Design for Living* (1933); *Idiot's Delight* (1936); *Amphitryon 38* (1937); *There Shall Be No Night* (1940); *O Mistress Mine* (1946; called *Love in Idleness* when they created it in London in 1944); *The Great Sebastians* (1956); and *The Visit* (1958). **215 & 216. LYNN FONTANNE** (ca. 1885–1983; born in England). On stage, provinces and London, 1905, as a protégée of Ellen Terry. First in U.S. (including N.Y.), 1910. In original London production of *My Lady's Dress* (1914). Back to U.S. (to stay), 1916, with Laurette Taylor; in *Out There* with her (1917). Success in *Dulcy* (1921). Most important role without Lunt: original Nina Leeds in *Strange Interlude* (1928). For their plays together, see no. 214.

217. JOSEPH SCHILDKRAUT (1895–1964; born in Vienna). To U.S. with father Rudolf Schildkraut, 1911; debut, N.Y., 1913. In Germany (including work with Max Reinhardt), 1913–20. Adult N.Y. debut, 1921. In *Liliom* (1921; with Eva Le Gallienne) and *The Firebrand* (1924). Managed the Hollywood Playhouse, 1927 ff. With the Civic Repertory Company, N.Y., 1932 (Queen of Hearts in *Alice in Wonderland*). Later N.Y. plays: *Uncle Harry* (1942; once more with Le Gallienne) and *The Diary of Anne Frank* (1955; played Mr. Frank to 1958; last in N.Y.). Oscar for film *The Life of Emile Zola*, 1937. **218.** William **CLAUDE RAINS** (1889–1967; born in England). London debut, 1900. Toured U.S., 1914/5, as general manager for Granville-Barker. Enormous London career in all sorts of plays. N.Y., 1926, in *The Constant Nymph*. Later N.Y. plays: *And So to Bed* (1928); *The Apple Cart* (1930); *Too True to Be Good* (1932); *The Man Who Reclaimed His Head* (1932); *The Good Earth* (1932); *They Shall Not Die* (1934); *Darkness at Noon* (1951); *The Confidential Clerk* (1954); and *The Night of the Auk* (1956; last N.Y.). Active elsewhere to 1965. **219. ARTHUR** William **BYRON** (1872–1943; son of Kate and Oliver Doud Byron; nephew of Ada Rehan, no. 50). Debut with father, 1889; N.Y., 1890. Acted with John Drew, Amelia Bingham, Mary Mannering, Maxine Elliott, Maude Adams and Ethel Barrymore. Long career in popular current plays. Outstanding in *The Criminal Code* (1929) and *Five Star Final* (1930). In 1936: in Cornell's *Saint Joan* revival, and Polonius in Gielgud's N.Y. *Hamlet*. Last N.Y. play, 1939.

220

221

220. James Ridley **OSGOOD PERKINS** (1892–1937; father of Anthony Perkins). Produced films together with Glenn Hunter and Roland Young before they persuaded him to go on stage in the N.Y. play *Beggar on Horseback* (1924). Brilliant comedy work in *The Front Page* (1928; role in photo) and *Goodbye Again* (1932). In Noël Coward's misbegotten *Point Valaine* with the Lunts (1935). Died after the first night of the Washington tryout of *Susan and God*. **221. HENRY TRAVERS** (1874–1965; born in England). Debut in England, 1895; London suburbs, 1898; N.Y., 1901. Much stock and touring before real N.Y. career began in 1917. A pillar of the Theatre Guild from 1919 to 1932 in such plays as: *Heartbreak House* (1920); *Liliom* (1921); *He Who Gets Slapped* and *From Morn Till Midnight* (both 1922); *Saint Joan* (1923); *Marco Millions* (1928); *Reunion in Vienna* (1931); and *The Good Earth* (1932). Greatest success as the cheerful patriarch in *You Can't Take It with You* (1936–38; last N.Y. play). Long film career.

222

223

224

222. HELEN GAHAGAN (1900–1980; married Melvyn Douglas, 1931). On stage, 1922; in N.Y. that year. In: *Chains* (1923); *Young Woodley* (1925); and the 1927 revival of *Trelawny of the "Wells."* Toured Europe in opera, 1928–30. U.S. singing roles in: *Tonight or Never* (N.Y.; 1930; Belasco's last production); the West Coast company of *The Cat and the Fiddle* (1932); etc. In the N.Y. play *Moor Born* (1934; as Emily Brontë). Last N.Y. play, 1952; last play, 1955; concerts and readings to 1962. Elected to U.S. House of Representatives from California in 1944, 1946 and 1948, she was defeated in her 1950 Senate race by Richard M. Nixon; she later served in distinguished political appointments. **223. ZITA JOHANN** (born 1904 in Hungary). N.Y. debut, 1924, in the Theatre Guild's *Man and the Masses*. Outstanding in *Machinal* (1928; with Clark Gable). In Philip Barry's *Tomorrow and Tomorrow* (1931). Last N.Y. play, 1942. Films. **224. RUTH DRAPER** (1884–1956). One of the most eminent American actresses, she appeared in only one standard N.Y. play, *A Lady's Name*, in 1916 (her first stage appearance was 1915). Beginning in London in 1920, she concentrated exclusively on monodrama, performing her own intelligent, humane and literate texts. Touring constantly, she gave at least a dozen N.Y. recitals from 1926 to 1956; she died during her last N.Y. engagement.

226

227

225. George **MELVILLE COOPER** (1896–1973; born in England).
Debut, 1914, at Stratford-upon-Avon. With the great Birmingham Repertory Company, 1920–24. London debut, 1924; in *The Farmer's Wife* (1924) and *Journey's End* (1929). N.Y. debut, 1935, in *Laburnum Grove*. In: Cole Porter's *Jubilee* (1935; he had been in London musicals); Weill's *The Firebrand of Florence* (1945); and *An Inspector Calls* (1947). Acted in California in later 1950s. Joined the cast of *My Fair Lady* in N.Y., 1959 (as Pickering; show opened 1956). Last N.Y. play, 1966. **226. ROLAND YOUNG** (1887–1953; born in England). Debut, 1908, London; N.Y., 1912. With Washington Square Players. Delightful suave comedian in: *Good Gracious Annabelle* (1916); *Beggar on Horseback* (1924); and *The Last of Mrs. Cheyney* (1925). Away from stage, 1928–33. Last N.Y. play, 1943; active in London to at least 1947. Many famous film roles, especially in Topper series. **227. JACOB BEN-AMI** (real surname, Shtchirin; 1890–1977; born in Russia). Began acting in Minsk, ca. 1907. To U.S., 1914, acting only in Yiddish until 1920, when he made his English-speaking debut with the encouragement of producer Arthur Hopkins. With Theatre Guild, 1923 ff. (in O'Neill's *Welded*, 1924). With Civic Repertory, 1929–31, in Chekhov, Tolstoy and Shakespeare. From 1934 to 1959, no acting on Broadway (but directed there, and acted in Chicago and elsewhere, both in English and in Yiddish). Back to N.Y., 1959, in *The Tenth Man*. Last N.Y. play, 1967.

228. Gladys Cooper and Philip Merivale (real-life man and wife) in *Call It a Day*, 1936. **GLADYS COOPER** (1888–1971; born in England). Debut in musicals: provinces, 1905; London, 1906. First regular play in London, 1911. Splendid, varied career; in: *My Lady's Dress* (1914); *Home and Beauty* (Maugham; 1919); *The Last of Mrs. Cheyney* (1925). Managed the Playhouse (London), 1927–33; in Maugham's *The Letter* (1927) and *The Painted Veil* (1931). N.Y. debut, 1934. Outstanding in *The Chalk Garden* (1955) and *A Passage to India* (1962; her last in N.Y.). Active in London to year of death. Oscar for film *Now Voyager*, 1942. **PHILIP MERIVALE** (1886–1946; born in India). Debut, 1905, London, with the Benson Shakespearean company; acted with Tree, 1911 ff. To U.S. (including N.Y.), 1914, with Mrs. Patrick Campbell (first U.S. Higgins in *Pygmalion*). In: *Pollyanna* (Detroit, 1915; N.Y., 1916); *The Swan* (1923); *The Road to Rome* (1927); *Death Takes a Holiday* (1929); *Cynara* (1931); *Mary of Scotland* (1933); and *Valley Forge* (1934). His *Othello* and *Macbeth* with Gladys Cooper in 1935 were not epoch-making. Last N.Y. play, 1938.

229

231

230

229. ANN HARDING (real name, Dorothy Walton Gatley; 1902–1981). Debut, 1921, N.Y., with the Provincetown Players; on Broadway, same year. Worked, 1921–25, at the Hedgerow (near Philadelphia) with Jasper Deeter, in Detroit with Jessie Bonstelle, and in Chicago. In N.Y. plays: *Tarnish* (1923); *Stolen Fruit* (1925); *The Woman Disputed* (1926); and the great success *The Trial of Mary Dugan* (1927). Films, 1929–56; stage tours, takeovers of roles, tryouts; N.Y. play, 1964. **230. HELEN** Frances **CHANDLER** (1909–1965; married, 1935–40, to Bramwell Fletcher, no. 289). Debut, 1918, N.Y., in *Penrod*. In the cast of John Barrymore's *Richard III* (1920) and Lionel's *Macbeth* (1921); Ophelia in Basil Sydney's modern-dress *Hamlet* (1925). Also in: *The Constant Nymph* (1926); *Springtime for Henry* (1931); *Pride and Prejudice* (1935); *Lady Precious Stream* (1936); and the major revival of *Outward Bound* (1938; her last N.Y. play). Acted in West Coast plays to 1941. **231. JOSEPHINE HUTCHINSON** (born 1904). Debut, 1920, Seattle; there to 1923. Distinguished repertory in Washington, D.C., 1923–25. N.Y., 1925. With Le Gallienne's Civic Repertory, 1926–33 (title role in *Alice in Wonderland*, 1932). In stock, 1936. Films, 1917–64.

232

233

234

232. William **ALEXANDER KIRKLAND** (born 1908 in Mexico; married, 1942–44, to Gypsy Rose Lee). Debut, 1925, in Washington, D.C.; N.Y., same year. Worked, 1927 ff., with Jasper Deeter, Jessie Bonstelle and Stuart Walker. N.Y. plays included: *Wings Over Europe* (1928); *Marseilles* (1930); *Men in White* (1933) and *Gold Eagle Guy* (1934), both with the Group Theatre; the 1938 revival of *Outward Bound*; and *Junior Miss* (1941). Founded the Berkshire Playhouse, Stockbridge, 1933. Last N.Y. play, 1945. Art dealer from 1950. **233.** Stanislas Pascal **FRANCHOT TONE** (1905–1968; married, 1935–39, to Joan Crawford). Son of a leading industrialist, he made his debut in Buffalo stock, 1927; N.Y., same year. In plays for the Theatre Guild (*Red Rust*, 1929; *Hotel Universe*, 1930; *Green Grow the Lilacs*, 1931) and for its progressive offshoot, the Group Theatre (*The House of Connelly* and *1931*, both 1931; *Night Over Taos*, 1932). Chiefly in films thereafter, but in N.Y. premiere of *A Moon for the Misbegotten* (1957). Last N.Y. play, 1967. **234. JOHN CROMWELL** (1887–1979). Began in Cleveland stock, 1907; N.Y., 1910. In: *Little Women* (1912); *Major Barbara* (1915); *Lucky Sam McCarver* (1925); and *Gentlemen of the Press* (1928). No stage acting, with one exception (1942), from 1928 to 1951, when he won a Tony for *Point of No Return*. Later, in: *Sabrina Fair* (1953) and *Mary, Mary* (1961). At Guthrie Theatre, Minneapolis, 1963–65. Last play (and last N.Y.), 1971. Despite the brilliance of his acting career, he was perhaps even more significant as a director—of plays, from 1913 to at least 1963; of films, from 1928 to 1956.

235

236

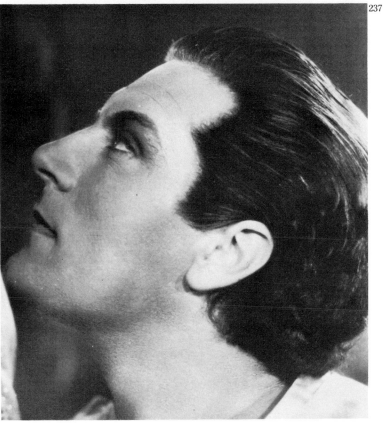

237

Three Englishmen on the American stage. **235. BRIAN** de Lacy **AHERNE** (born 1902; married, 1939–43, to Joan Fontaine). On stage, 1910, with the Pilgrim Players (who became the Birmingham Rep); London, 1913. Full stage activity from 1923 (had tried architecture). N.Y. debut, 1931, with Katharine Cornell in *The Barretts of Wimpole Street*. Continued with her in *Lucrece* (1932); *Romeo and Juliet* (1934; as Mercutio); and numerous revivals. In the national company of *My Fair Lady*, 1957/8. Back with Cornell on 1959/60 tour of *Dear Liar* (as GBS; N.Y., 1960). Plays in Florida and in London, 1965. **236. LESLIE HOWARD** (real surname, Stainer; 1893–1943). Debut, provinces, 1917; London, 1918; N.Y., 1920. N.Y. plays included: *The Truth About Blaydes* (1922); *Outward Bound* (1924); *The Green Hat* (1925); *Her Cardboard Lover* and *Escape* (both 1927); *Berkeley Square* (1929); *The Animal Kingdom* (1932); *The Petrified Forest* (1935); and his highly controversial *Hamlet* (1936; last in N.Y.). Participated in a patriotic pageant in London not long before his R.A.F. plane was shot down. **237. DENNIS KING** (1897–1971). With the Birmingham Repertory Company, 1916; London, 1919; N.Y., 1921, in *Clair de Lune*, with Ethel and John Barrymore. Long, varied, distinguished Broadway career included (* = musicals): *Back to Methuselah* (1922); Jane Cowl's *Romeo and Juliet* (1923; as Mercutio); *Rose-Marie* (1924;*); *The Vagabond King* (1925;*); *The Three Musketeers* (1928;*); *Richard of Bordeaux* (1934); *I Married an Angel* (1938;*); *Billy Budd* (1951); and *A Patriot for Me* (1969; last in N.Y.).

Three actresses often remembered for giddy roles, but capable of much more. **238. NYDIA** Eileen **WESTMAN** (1902–1970). Began in vaude with parents, 1913, Bronx, N.Y. Real N.Y. debut, 1924, in *Pigs*. In *The Merchant of Yonkers* (1938). Succeeded June Walker in the national tour of *Life with Father*, 1944, and joined the N.Y. company, same year. Later, in *The Madwoman of Chaillot* (1948) and *The Sleeping Prince* (1956). Last N.Y. play, 1961; last play, 1963.   **239. ALICE BRADY** (1892–1939; daughter of producer William Brady; stepdaughter of Grace George, no. 100). On stage, 1909, with Mantell; N.Y., 1910, in a *Mikado* chorus (she had studied for opera and was often in singing roles to 1915). In *Little Women* (1912). Long career, largely in standard Broadway fare, until her great creation of Lavinia Mannon in *Mourning Becomes Electra* (1931). Last N.Y. play, 1932; play in Los Angeles, 1934.   **240. MARY BOLAND** (1885–1965). Debut, 1901, Detroit; N.Y., 1905. As John Drew's leading lady at the Empire, 1908–13, she was in the two Maugham plays *Jack Straw* (1908) and *Smith* (1910). Later, in *My Lady's Dress* (1914) and *Clarence* (1919). Developed into brilliant comedienne in such plays as: *The Torch-Bearers* (1922); *The Cradle Snatchers* (1925); *Face the Music* (Berlin musical, 1932); and *Jubilee* (Porter musical, 1935). Last N.Y. play, 1954.

243

241. EUGÉNIE LEONTOVICH (born 1900 in Russia; married, 1923–46, to Gregory Ratoff). With Moscow Art Theatre; to Paris and other western European cities after Revolution. N.Y. debut, 1922, in the *Revue Russe* (difficult period of show choruses, tours, etc.). Great success as female lead in *Grand Hotel* (1930) and *Twentieth Century* (1932). Later, in *Dark Eyes* (1943) and *Anastasia* (1954). Own theater in Los Angeles, 1948–52. Taught there, 1953 ff.; in Chicago, 1963 ff. Latest N.Y. appearance, off-Broadway, 1972, in *Anna K.* **242. ANNE REVERE** (born 1903). Walk-on at the American Laboratory Theatre, N.Y., 1928. Stock with Stuart Walker and others. Broadway debut, 1931. In Lillian Hellman's *The Children's Hour* (1934). Much work out of N.Y.; for example, with the Surry (Me.) Players, 1937–39, and at the Phoenix-Westwood Theatre, Los Angeles, 1945. Tony, N.Y., 1960, for *Toys in the Attic*. Latest N.Y. play, 1966. Oscar for the film *National Velvet*, 1945. **243. ANN** Dorothea **SHOE-MAKER** (1891–1978). Debut in Philadelphia stock, 1909; N.Y., 1910. In: O'Neill's *The Great God Brown* (1926); *The Living Room* (1954); and the national companies of *The Bad Seed* (1955/6), *Separate Tables* (1957/8) and *Sunrise at Campobello* (1958–60; in part of N.Y. run as well). Last N.Y. play, 1965.

244. Charles **GLENN ANDERS** (1889–1981). Debut in Los Angeles stock, 1910; N.Y. stock, 1912; Broadway, 1919. In: *Hell-Bent fer Heaven* and *They Knew What They Wanted* (both 1924); *Strange Interlude* (1928); *Hotel Universe* (1930); *Moor Born* (1934; as Bramwell Brontë); *The Masque of Kings* (1937); and *Time Remembered* (1957; last in N.Y.). Active to at least 1960. **245. WALTER HUSTON** (1884–1950; born in Canada; father of John Huston). Debut, 1902, Toronto; N.Y., 1905. Vaudeville, 1909–24. Major N.Y. plays: O'Neill's *Desire Under the Elms* (1924) and *The Fountain* (1925); *The Barker* (1927); *Dodsworth* (1935); *Othello* (1937; not a success, though he had done the role since 1934, beginning in Central City, Colo.); Weill's *Knickerbocker Holiday* (1938); and *The Apple of His Eye* (1946; last N.Y.). **246. TOM POWERS** (1890–1955). Debut, 1911, in Pennsylvania, with Stuart Walker in N.Y., 1916. Broadway plays (from 1916) included: Kern's *Oh, Boy!* (1917; also in London cast, 1919); *Tarnish* (1923); *White Wings* (1926); *Strange Interlude* (1928); *The Apple Cart* (1930); *The Sailors of Cattaro* (1934); and *End of Summer* (1936). Last N.Y. play, 1944. **247. PAUL MUNI** (real name, Frederick Weisenfreund; 1895–1967; born in Austro-Hungarian Galicia). In Yiddish stock, N.Y., 1908; at the Yiddish Art Theatre, 1918–26. English-speaking N.Y. debut (as Muni Weisenfreund), 1926, in *We Americans*. "Paul Muni" from 1930. N.Y. successes: *Counsellor-at-Law* (1931; also in 1942 revival); *Key Largo* (1939); and *Inherit the Wind* (1955; won Tony; last in N.Y.). First Willy Loman in London (*Death of a Salesman*), 1949. Active on stage to at least 1958. Great film career; Oscar, 1936, for *The Story of Louis Pasteur*.

248

249

250

248. ESTELLE WINWOOD (née Goodwin; born 1883 in England). Debut, 1898, Manchester; London, 1899; with famous Liverpool Repertory Theatre, 1911 ff. N.Y. debut, 1916. Most important plays: *Why Marry?* (1917; first Pulitzer Prize play); *The Circle* (1921); *The Chief Thing* (1926); *Fallen Angels* (1927); *Ladies in Retirement* (1940); *The Pirate* (1942); revival of *Lady Windermere's Fan* (1946); and *The Madwoman of Chaillot* (1948). Last N.Y. play, 1966. **249. CARROLL McCOMAS** (ca. 1886–1962). Debut, 1905, in a N.Y. musical. Though she was in a rich variety of N.Y. plays to 1950, no other part of hers was as significant as the title role in the 1920 *Miss Lulu Bett*, a Broadway milestone. **250. MADY CHRISTIANS** (real given names, Marguerita Maria; 1900–1951; born in Austria; daughter of eminent actor Rudolph Christians). To N.Y. with her parents, 1912; acted in German at the Irving Place Theatre. Back to Austria, 1917; worked with Reinhardt. Permanent residence in U.S. from 1931. Broadway debut, 1933. In 1938, Gertrude in Maurice Evans' *Hamlet*; 1939, in his *Henry IV, Part 1*. Also in *Watch on the Rhine* (1941) and as Mama in *I Remember Mama* (1944). Last N.Y. play, 1949. Acted on West Coast, 1950.

251. DOROTHY GISH (1898–1968; sister of Lillian Gish; married, 1920–35, to James Rennie, no. 200). Debut, 1902; N.Y., 1903. Chief segment of film career, 1912–28. Back in N.Y. as adult, 1928. In: *Morning's at Seven* (1939) and *Love for Love* revival (1940; role in photo). Succeeded Dorothy Stickney in *Life with Father* in 1940. Later, in *The Magnificent Yankee* (1946) and *The Man* (1956; last in N.Y.). In plays elsewhere to 1956. **252. LILLIAN GISH** (born 1893; sister of Dorothy Gish). On stage, 1902. Her first N.Y. play was *A Good Little Devil* (1913), and the next—following the most fabulous part of her film career—was *Uncle Vanya* (1930; role in photo). Later N.Y. plays: *Within the Gates* (1934); Gielgud's *Hamlet* (1936; as Ophelia); *The Star Wagon* (1937); *All the Way Home* (1960); *Anya* (1965; musical); and *I Never Sang for My Father* (1968). Latest N.Y. appearance, 1975/6, in a musical. At Stratford, Conn., 1965. **253. MARGARET WEBSTER** (1905–1972; born in N.Y. of English parents, the actors Ben Webster and May Whitty). On stage, Chiswick (Eng.), 1917; London, 1924. In cast of John Barrymore's London *Hamlet* (1925). At Old Vic, 1929/30. Began directing (her principal career), 1935. First in N.Y. as director, 1937 (Evans' *Richard II*). Acting in N.Y. included: revivals of *The Seagull* and *The Three Sisters* (1938); *Family Portrait* (1939); potted Shakespeare at the World's Fair (1939); and the role of Emilia in the Robeson *Othello* (1943). Connected with American Repertory Theatre, N.Y., 1946/7. Own Shakespeare company, 1948–50. One-woman recitals, 1963 to at least 1966.

254

254. Julie Haydon and Eddie Dowling in *The Time of Your Life*, 1939. **JULIE HAYDON** (real name, Donella Lightfoot Donaldson; born 1910; married critic George Jean Nathan, 1955). Acted on West Coast, 1929–34; Titania in Reinhardt's Hollywood Bowl *Midsummer Night's Dream*, 1934. N.Y. debut, 1935. Came to the fore in *Shadow and Substance* (1938). Greatest role: in *The Glass Menagerie* (Chicago, 1944; N.Y., 1945). Latest N.Y. play, 1947; active to at least 1962. **EDDIE DOWLING** (real name, Joseph Nelson Goucher; 1894–1976; married to comedienne Ray Dooley). Debut, 1909, Providence; N.Y., 1919. Earlier career in musicals: *Ziegfeld Follies* (1919, 1920); *Honeymoon Lane* (1926); *Thumbs Up!* (1934). Began producing important plays, 1937, with the Evans *Richard II* (also became a major director). Straight acting in N.Y. began 1939 (in *The Time of Your Life*). In *The Glass Menagerie* with Julie Haydon and Laurette Taylor. Succeeded James Barton in the musical *Paint Your Wagon*, 1952 (last N.Y. appearance). In 1961, founded the Eddie Dowling University Theatre Foundation at Florida State University. **255. FRANK CRAVEN** (1875–1945; father of actor John Craven). An actor's son, he went on stage in 1887. N.Y. debut, 1907. In: *Bought and Paid For* (1911); *Going Up* (1917; musical); *The First Year* (1920; he was author); and *Our Town* (1937; as Stage Manager—his best part). Last N.Y. play, 1944.

Three stars of the Group Theatre. **256. MORRIS CARNOVSKY** (born 1897). In acting groups from 1914. N.Y. debut, 1922, in *God of Vengeance*. With Theatre Guild, 1923–30 (in: *Saint Joan*, 1923; *Marco Millions*, 1928; etc.); then in its leftwing offshoot, the Group Theatre, 1931–40 (in: *Men in White*, 1933; *Awake and Sing*, 1935; *Golden Boy*, 1937; etc.). Later, in *My Sister Eileen* (1940), *Rhinoceros* (1961) and a host of other plays, in N.Y. and around the country (including Actors Laboratory Theatre, Hollywood), to at least 1970. At Stratford, Conn., 1956–70. **257. STELLA ADLER** (born 1902; sister of Luther Adler, no. 258; cousin of Francine Larrimore, no. 209; married, 1943–60, to Harold Clurman). Began acting in Yiddish at age 4 with eminent father Jacob Adler; with him to 1920. On Broadway in English, 1922, as Lola Adler. With experimental American Laboratory Theatre, 1926, as Stella Adler. Seasons with Bertha Kalich, Jacob Ben-Ami and Maurice Schwartz (1930, at his Yiddish Art Theatre, N.Y.). Into the Group Theatre, 1931 (in: *Night Over Taos*, 1932; *Gold Eagle Guy*, 1934; *Awake and Sing*, 1935; etc.). Latest N.Y. play, 1946; play in London, 1961. Still teaching acting at her own school, N.Y., 1983. **258. LUTHER ADLER** (first name actually Lutha; born 1903; married, 1938–47, to Sylvia Sidney). On stage with father Jacob Adler at age 5. English-speaking debut, 1921, with Provincetown Players. On Broadway, 1923, in *Humoresque*. In *Red Rust* for the Guild, 1929. Into Group plays, including: *Men in White* (1933); *Awake and Sing* and *Waiting for Lefty* (both 1935); *Golden Boy* (1937; lead role); and *Thunder Rock* (1939). Subsequently, much work out of N.Y. (tours with Sylvia Sidney in 1940s). Back in N.Y., 1956–65. Toured in *Fiddler on the Roof*, 1966.

260

261

259. Margo and Henry Hull in *The Masque of Kings*, 1937.
MARGO (María Margarita Guadalupe Bolado y Castilla; born
1920 in Mexico). On stage at age 10 in Los Angeles. Famous
N.Y. debut in *Winterset*, 1935. Also in *A Bell for Adano* (1944).
Later, in stock and out of N.Y. Gave dance concerts in Mexico
City, 1940. **HENRY HULL** (1890–1977; brother-in-law of
Margaret Anglin, no. 84, and of Josephine Hull, no. 296). Debut, 1909, Pittsburgh; N.Y., 1911, with Anglin. In: *The Cat and
the Canary* (1922); *Lulu Belle* (1926); *Grand Hotel* (1930); and
the long-running *Tobacco Road* (1933; the original Jeeter Lester). Last N.Y. play, 1959. **260. RUTH GORDON** (actually,
Ruth Gordon Jones; born 1896; first husband, Gregory Kelly,
no. 170; married Garson Kanin in 1942). Debut, 1915, N.Y.,
with Maude Adams in a *Peter Pan* revival. Indianapolis stock
with Gregory Kelly; with him in *Seventeen* (1918) in N.Y. Later
successes include: *Saturday's Children* (1927); *Serena Blandish*
(1929); *Hotel Universe* (1930); *They Shall Not Die* (1934); *Ethan
Frome* (1936); *The Country Wife* (also 1936; earlier, in London);
Over 21 (1944; she was author); and *The Matchmaker* (1954;
N.Y., 1955). Latest N.Y. play, 1976. One of the great ladies of
our stage. **261. BURGESS MEREDITH** (born 1908; married, 1944–50, to Paulette Goddard). Apprenticeship with Eva
Le Gallienne, N.Y.; debut with her, 1929; with her to 1932
(Dormouse in *Alice in Wonderland*, that year). Noteworthy in
Little Old Boy and *She Loves Me Not* (both 1933). Fame in
Winterset (1935). Also in *High Tor* and *The Star Wagon* (both
1937) and *The Remarkable Mr. Pennypacker* (1953). Latest N.Y.
acting, 1964; in Los Angeles, 1975. Very active director: latest
job, 1980, Pittsburgh.

262. Violet Heming and Romney Brent in the Players' revival of *Love for Love*, 1940. **VIOLET HEMING** (1895–1981; born in England). U.S. debut, 1908; N.Y., same year. Toured with Arliss, 1912–14. N.Y. plays included: *Three Faces East* (1918); *Spring Cleaning* (1923); *There's Always Juliet* (1932); and *Yes, My Darling Daughter* (1937). Last Broadway play, 1952; off-Broadway to 1964. **ROMNEY BRENT** (real name, Rómulo Larralde, Jr.; 1902–1976; born in Mexico). Debut, 1922, N.Y., in *He Who Gets Slapped*. Remained with Theatre Guild, on and off, to mid-1930s; in: the first *Garrick Gaieties* (1925) and *The Warrior's Husband* (1932). London activity included Coward's revue *Words and Music* (1932), in which he introduced "Mad Dogs and Englishmen," and the book and direction of Porter's *Nymph Errant* (1933). In N.Y., later, was in *Joan of Lorraine* (1946) and took over the male role in *The Fourposter* in 1952. In a New Haven tryout, 1962.

263. SIR (Arthur) **JOHN GIELGUD** (knighted 1963; English; born 1904; grandnephew of Ellen Terry, no. 42). Debut at Old Vic, 1921; major roles there, 1929–31. Incredibly rich London career as actor and director. N.Y. acting appearances began 1928, in *The Patriot*; continued with a wildly acclaimed *Hamlet*, 1936; and later included *The Lady's Not for Burning* (1950; he had created male lead role, London, 1949); the Shakespeare recital *The Ages of Man* (1958 and 1963); *Five Finger Exercise* (1959); *Tiny Alice* (1964); *Home* (1970); and *No Man's Land* (1976; his latest in N.Y.). **264. RAYMOND** Hart **MASSEY** (1896–1983; born in Canada). Debut, 1922, London. Varied career there, including management, before N.Y. debut as Hamlet, 1931. Other N.Y. plays: *Ethan Frome* (1936); *Abe Lincoln in Illinois* (1938; huge success); and *J. B.* (1958; last in N.Y.). Play in London, 1970; acted in Los Angeles in 1975/6 season. **265. SIR CEDRIC** Webster **HARDWICKE** (knighted 1934; English; 1893–1964). Amateur from 1905; professional debut in London, 1912; at Birmingham Rep, 1922–24. British creations included: *The Farmer's Wife* (1924); *The Apple Cart* (1929); *The Barretts of Wimpole Street* (1930); and *Too True to be Good* (1932). N.Y. debut, 1936. Major N.Y. plays: *The Amazing Dr. Clitterhouse* (1937); *Shadow and Substance* (1938); revival of *Caesar and Cleopatra* (1949); and *A Majority of One* (1959; ran to 1961; last in N.Y.). **266.** Judith Anderson and Maurice Evans in a TV *Macbeth*, 1954. **DAME JUDITH ANDERSON** (real name, Frances Margaret Anderson-Anderson; born 1898 in Australia). Debut, 1915, Sydney. To U.S. (including N.Y.), 1918: toured with Gillette, 1920. Slinky temptress in *Cobra* (1924) and *The Dove* (1925). Tours and N.Y. takeovers in *Strange Interlude* (1928/9) and *Mourning Becomes Electra* (1932). Later, in N.Y.: *The Old Maid* (1935); Gertrude in Gielgud's *Hamlet* (1936); *The Tower Beyond Tragedy* (1940, Carmel; 1950, N.Y.); *Macbeth* with Evans, 1941; and *Medea* (1947 as Medea; 1982 as the Nurse—her latest in N.Y.). In 1971, two nights in N.Y. in title role of *Hamlet*. **MAURICE** Herbert **EVANS** (born 1901 in England). Debut, 1926, Cambridge; London, 1927. In *Journey's End* (1928/9) and at Old Vic (1934/5). N.Y. debut as Romeo with Cornell, 1935 (after the tour). Later, in N.Y.: *St. Helena* (1936); *Richard II* (1937); *Hamlet* (1938); the "G.I. *Hamlet*" (1945/6); *The Browning Version* (1949); *Dial "M" for Murder* (1952); *Tenderloin* (1960; musical); and *The Aspern Papers* (1962; latest in N.Y.). In Los Angeles, 1965/6; Washington, D.C., 1973; Nova Scotia, 1979.

267. Katharine Cornell and Edith Evans in *Romeo and Juliet*, 1934. **KATHARINE CORNELL** (1893–1974; born in Berlin of American parents; was married to director Guthrie McClintic). Debut, 1916, with Washington Square Players. First acting in London, 1919. Broadway plays to 1930 included: *Nice People* and *A Bill of Divorcement* (both 1921); *The Enchanted Cottage* (1923); *Candida* revival (1924); *The Green Hat* (1925); and *The Letter* (1927). As actress/manager, in: *The Barretts of Wimpole Street* (1931); *Alien Corn* (1933); *Romeo and Juliet* (1933–35; huge tour; first N.Y., 1934); *The Wingless Victory* (1936); *No Time for Comedy* (1939); *Antony and Cleopatra* (1947); *That Lady* (1949); *The Dark Is Light Enough* (1955); and *Dear Liar* (1959; N.Y., 1960; her last there). **DAME EDITH EVANS** (English; 1888–1976). Probably the most distinguished 20th-century English actress. Came to public attention, 1912, in the Elizabethan Stage Society. West End debut, 1913. Her first Millamant in *The Way of the World*, 1924; her first Nurse in *Romeo and Juliet*, 1925, at the Old Vic. In premiere of *The Apple Cart* (1929). London appearances up to the 1973/4 season. N.Y. appearances: 1931 (in *The Lady with a Lamp*);

1933; 1934 (as the Nurse); 1950 (in *Daphne Laureola*); and 1964 (in the program *Homage to Shakespeare* at Philharmonic Hall). **268. DONALD COOK** (1901–1961). Vaudeville and Kansas City community theater before professional debut, 1925, in a tour with Mrs. Fiske. N.Y. debut, 1926. In N.Y. plays: *Paris Bound* (1927); *Wine of Choice* (1938); *Skylark* (1939); *Claudia* (1941); *Foolish Notion* (1945); *Private Lives* revival (1948; had toured in it with Tallulah, 1946); and *The Moon is Blue* (1951). Last N.Y. play, 1961. **269. TALLULAH** Brockman **BANKHEAD** (1902–1968; married, 1937–41, to actor John Emery). Debut, 1918, N.Y.: in *Nice People* (1921). Successful London career, 1923–30, included the creation of *Fallen Angels* and *The Green Hat* (both 1925) and local versions of Broadway hits. Back to U.S., 1933. N.Y. plays included: *Dark Victory* (1934); *The Little Foxes* (1939; role in photo; her greatest triumph); *The Skin of Our Teeth* (1942); *Foolish Notion* (1945); *The Eagle Has Two Heads* (1947); and a revival of Tennessee Williams' *The Milk Train Doesn't Stop Here Anymore* (1964; her last in N.Y.).

270

271

272

273

274

275

106

276

270. William **RUSSELL HARDIE** (1904–1973). Debut, 1925, Buffalo; N.Y., 1929, in *The Criminal Code*. In *Pagan Lady* (1930) and *Home of the Brave* (1945). Active on Broadway to early 1960s. **271. RUSSELL** Henry **COLLINS** (born 1897). Debut, 1922, at Cleveland Playhouse; there 10 years. N.Y. plays from 1932, including: *Both Your Houses* (1933); Group Theatre work, as in *Waiting for Lefty* (1935) and Weill's *Johnny Johnson* (1936; title role); *The Star Wagon* (1937); *Here Come the Clowns* (1938); *Morning's at Seven* (1939); *The Moon Is Down* (1942); *Carousel* (1945); *The Iceman Cometh* (1946); and *A View from the Bridge* (1955). Latest in N.Y., 1959; active to at least 1965. **272. ENID** Virginia **MARKEY** (ca. 1890–1981). N.Y. debut, 1919, in *Up in Mabel's Room*. In: *The Women* (1936); *Morning's at Seven* (1939); *Mrs. McThing* (1952); and *The Ballad of the Sad Café* (1963). Last N.Y. play, 1967. Interesting film career: with W. S. Hart, 1915; first film Jane (Tarzan's mate), 1918. **273. CAROL** Marie **GOODNER** (born 1904). Debut at 4 in tour; vaudeville. In 1923 edition of Berlin's *Music Box Revue*; in *The Great Gatsby* (1926). Varied roles in London, 1927–29 and 1931–38. Back in N.Y.: *The Man Who Came to Dinner* (1939; as Lorraine Sheldon); succeeded Eve Arden in *Let's Face It* in 1942; *Deep Are the Roots* (1945); *The Cocktail Party* (1950); *The Living Room* (1954); and *A Man for All Seasons* (1961; latest in N.Y.). **274. COLIN KEITH-JOHNSTON** (English; born 1896). London debut, 1919. With Birmingham Rep, 1921–25. N.Y. debut,

1929, repeating London role in *Journey's End*. Laertes in Massey's *Hamlet* (1931). Also in: *Dangerous Corner* (1932); *Pride and Prejudice* (1935); *The Autumn Garden* and *Point of No Return* (both 1951). Latest N.Y. play, 1956. **275. WILLIAM HARRIGAN** (1893–1966; son of Edward Harrigan of Harrigan & Hart; brother of Nedda Harrigan Logan). In 1898 N.Y. revival of his father's *Reilly and the 400*. Later, in: *The Dove* (1925); O'Neill's *The Great God Brown* (1926; title role); *The Animal Kingdom* (1932); *Dear Ruth* (1944); and *Mister Roberts* (1948; as the Captain). Last N.Y. play, 1957. **276.** Aline MacMahon and Wallace Ford in *Kindred*, 1939. **ALINE MacMAHON** (born 1899). This unbelievably gifted and versatile actress made her professional debut at the Neighborhood Playhouse, N.Y., in 1921. The next year, she succeeded Winifred Lenihan in *The Dover Road* on Broadway. Later highlights: *Maya* (1928); *Once in a Lifetime* (1931); *The Eve of St. Mark* (1942); *The Confidential Clerk* (1954); and *All the Way Home* (1960). In *The Madwoman of Chaillot* in Washington, D.C., 1961; at Stratford, Conn., 1965. Has appeared in N.Y. (often at Lincoln Center) up to 1975. **WALLACE FORD** (real name, Samuel Jones; 1898–1966; born in England). In stock in Winnipeg as a boy. N.Y. debut, 1918, in the run of *Seventeen*. Greatest role: George in *Of Mice and Men* (1937). Succeeded Sidney Blackmer in *Come Back, Little Sheba* for 8 weeks in 1950 (last in N.Y.).

277. Frank Conroy and Peter Holden while in *On Borrowed Time*, 1938.   **FRANK CONROY** (1890–1964; born in England). Debut, 1908; London, 1910; N.Y. , 1914. Organized and built the Greenwich Village Theatre, 1916; there in repertory to 1919. Major N.Y. plays: *The Bad Man* (1920); *In a Garden* (1925); *On Borrowed Time* (1938; as Mr. Brink); *The Little Foxes* (1939; as Horace Giddens); *Point of No Return* (1951); and *The Potting Shed* (1957). Last N.Y. play, 1962.   **PETER HOLDEN** (Peter Holden Parkhurst; born 1931). Was on radio in 1936. Amazing feat in *On Borrowed Time* (1938); the producers thought that 3 boys would need to rotate in the taxing role, but he did most of the performances (not opening night). A brief flurry of filming after that play.   **278. SIDNEY BLACKMER** (1895–1973; married in 1930s to Lenore Ulric, no. 130). Debut, 1917, N.Y. In Ben Greet's Shakespearean troupe, 1917; in Maxine Elliott's last play, 1920. Success in *The Mountain Man* (1921); great acclaim in *Come Back, Little Sheba* (1950; Tony award). In *Sweet Bird of Youth* (1959) and *A Case of Libel* (1963; last in N.Y.). Active in 1965. Besides acting, he was a mining executive in North Carolina.

280

279

281

279. ROBERT KEITH (Robert Keith Rickey; born 1898). Debut, 1914, in stock in Illinois. N.Y., 1921. Highlights: *The Great God Brown* (1926; as Dion Anthony); with Civic Repertory (1933); *Yellow Jack* and *The Children's Hour* (both 1934); *Tortilla Flat* (1938); *Kiss and Tell* (1943); and *Mister Roberts* (1948; as Doc; his last in N.Y.). Films into 1960s. **280. ROBERT WARWICK** (real name, Robert Taylor Bien; 1878–1964). Studied for opera. Debut, N.Y., 1903, as understudy. In *The Balkan Princess* (1911; operetta; Alice Brady's first show with a role). Solid N.Y. career, including interesting revivals, to 1929. Continued stage work on West Coast during busy film career, appearing last in 1944 in Los Angeles and Chicago. **281. LEO G. CARROLL** (1892–1972; born in England). Debut, 1911, provinces; London, 1912. First in N.Y., 1912; regularly from 1924. In: *The Vortex* (1925); *The Constant Nymph* (1926); *Too True to Be Good* (1932); *The Green Bay Tree* (1933); *The Masque of Kings* (1937); *Angel Street* (1941; as the police inspector); and *The Late George Apley* (1944). Last N.Y., 1956; last of all, 1959.

109

282. WALTER ABEL (born 1898). In N.Y. student play, 1918; professional N.Y. debut, 1919; Broadway debut, 1922, in *Back to Methuselah*. In Provincetown Players' revival of *Fashion* (1924); same year, in *Desire Under the Elms*. After touring as Orin Mannon in *Mourning Becomes Electra*, took over role in N.Y., 1932. Also in: *The Wingless Victory* (1936); *The Wisteria Trees* (1950); and *The Pleasure of His Company* (1958). Latest N.Y. appearance, 1978. **283. HIRAM SHERMAN** (born 1908). Amateur work in Illinois, 1922; Chicago repertory at Goodman Theatre, 1927/8. Associated with Orson Welles in N.Y., 1936–38; in: *Horse Eats Hat* (1936); *The Cradle Will Rock* and the *Julius Caesar* revival (both 1937); and *The Shoemaker's Holiday* (1938; role in photo). Later, in: *Sing Out the News* (1938) and *Very Warm for May* (1939; both musicals); José Ferrer's *Cyrano de Bergerac* (1946) and *The Alchemist* (1948); and *How Now, Dow Jones* (1967; Tony award; his last in N.Y.). Still active, 1971. At Stratford, Conn., 1956, 1958, 1959 and 1961. **284. ELLIOTT** John **NUGENT** (1899–1980; son of actor John C. Nugent). Debut at age 4 in parents' vaudeville act. Real debut, 1919, Milwaukee, with Stuart Walker. N.Y. debut, 1921, in *Dulcy*. Was co-author as well as actor in: *Kempy* (1922); *The Poor Nut* (1925); and *The Male Animal* (1940; written with James Thurber; Nugent was also in the 1952 N.Y. revival). Biggest hit: the long-running *The Voice of the Turtle* (1943). Last N.Y. acting, succeeding Tom Ewell in *The Seven Year Itch* in 1954. In a tryout, 1956. Also major director of plays and films.

283

284

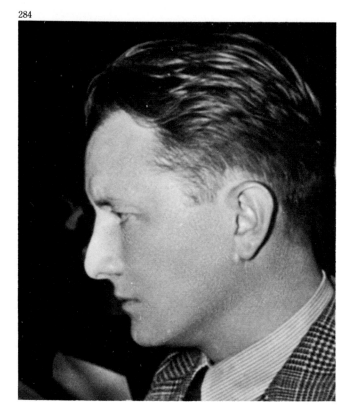

285. SAM LEVENE (real surname, Levine; 1905–1980; born in Russia). N.Y. debut, 1927. In: *Dinner at Eight* (1932); *Yellow Jack* (1934); *Three Men on a Horse* (1935); *Room Service* (1937); *Margin for Error* (1939); *Light Up the Sky* (1948); *Guys and Dolls* (1950; musical); *The Sunshine Boys* (1972); and a revival of *The Royal Family* (1975). Last N.Y. appearance in the year of his death. **286. JOHN HALLI-DAY** (1880–1947). American, grew up in England. Onto U.S. stage touring with Nat Goodwin. In N.Y. by 1912; stock in Cleveland, San Francisco and Denver, 1912–18, then regularly in N.Y. to 1934. In: *The Circle* (1921); *East of Suez* (1922); and *Rain from Heaven* (1934; also did this in Chicago, 1935). **287. MYRON McCORMICK** (1908–1962). Member of the University Players on Cape Cod in the late 1920s, along with Henry Fonda, Margaret Sullavan, Joshua Logan and many other soon-to-be-famous actors. N.Y. debut, 1932. Plays included: *Yellow Jack* (1934); *The Wingless Victory* (1936); *Thunder Rock* (1939); *State of the Union* (1945); *South Pacific* (1949; as Luther Billis); and *No Time for Sergeants* (1955; his last in N.Y.).

288. Florence Eldridge and Fredric March (they married in 1927). **FLORENCE ELDRIDGE** (born 1901). Debut, 1918, in a N.Y. chorus. In: *The Cat and the Canary* and *Six Characters in Search of an Author* (both 1922) and *The Great Gatsby* (1926). Toured with her husband in Theatre Guild plays, 1927/8; appeared with him on Broadway in: *The Skin of Our Teeth* (1942); *The Autumn Garden* (1951); and their greatest effort, O'Neill's *Long Day's Journey into Night* (1956; her latest in N.Y.). They gave concert readings in Europe and the Middle East in 1965.   **FREDRIC MARCH** (real name, Frederick McIntyre Bickel; 1897–1975). Debut, 1920, Baltimore; same year, in N.Y., in *Deburau*. Billed as Fred Bickel to 1924. In addition to co-appearances with his wife (see above), his N.Y. plays included: *The Devil in the Cheese* (1926); *A Bell for Adano* (1944); and *Gideon* (1961; his last in N.Y.). He won a Tony for *Long Day's Journey*, and Oscars for his films *Dr. Jekyll and Mr. Hyde* (1932) and *The Best Years of Our Lives* (1947).   **289. BRAMWELL FLETCHER** (born 1904 in England; was married to Helen Chandler, no. 230, and to Diana Barrymore). Debut, 1927, at Stratford-upon-Avon; London, same year; N.Y., 1929. In: *Within the Gates* (1934); *Lady Precious Stream* (1936); revival of *Outward Bound* (1938); and *Margin for Error* (1939). Much touring; in many high-class revivals. Played Higgins over 200 times during original N.Y. run of *My Fair Lady*, 1956–61. Toured in one-man shows, 1962–65 (including N.Y.). In *The Miser*, Chicago, 1967.   **290. HELEN HAYES** (Helen Hayes Brown; born 1900; married, 1928–56, to playwright Charles MacArthur). Debut, 1905, Washington, D.C.; N.Y., 1909, in *Old Dutch*, with Lew Fields; with him to 1911. Later N.Y. plays include: *Penrod* and *Dear Brutus* (both 1918); *Clarence* (1919); *To the Ladies* (1922); revival of *What Every Woman Knows* (1926); *Coquette* (1927; a great personal triumph); *Mary of Scotland* (1933); *Victoria Regina* (1935; role in photo; her biggest success); *Happy Birthday* (1947; Tony award); *The Wisteria Trees* (1950); *Mrs.*

McThing (1952); *Time Remembered* (1957); and *A Touch of the Poet* (1958). Own repertory company, 1964. Latest N.Y. play, 1970. Oscar, 1931, for film *The Sin of Madelon Claudet.* Commonly referred to as "the first lady of the American theater."

291. LEE J. COBB (= Lee Jacob; 1911–1976). Acted in Pasadena, 1929–33. In N.Y., from 1935, associated with Group Theatre and other politically liberal production firms; in: *Crime and Punishment* and *Waiting for Lefty* (both 1935); *Bitter Stream* and Weill's *Johnny Johnson* (both 1936); and *Golden Boy* (1937; also in 1952 revival). Role of lifetime: Willy Loman in *Death of a Salesman* (1949). Last N.Y. appearance as King Lear, 1968. **292. KARL MALDEN** (real name, Mladew Sekulovich; born 1914). N.Y. debut, 1937, in *Golden Boy*. Also in: *Key Largo* (1939); *Uncle Harry* (1942); *Winged Victory* (1943); *Truckline Café* (1946); *All My Sons* and *A Streetcar Named Desire* (both 1947); and *The Desperate Hours* (1955). Last N.Y. play, 1957. Since 1947, much screen and TV work; Oscar, 1952, for movie version of *Streetcar*. **293. LOUIS CALHERN** (real name, Carl Henry Vogt; 1895–1956). On stage in N.Y. stock, 1912. In St. Louis stock, 1914–16; with Anglin, 1916. Regular N.Y. career from 1922, including: *Cobra* (1924); *In a Garden* (1925); and *The Woman Disputed* (1926). Toured in *Life with Father*, 1941/2, and took over main role in N.Y., 1942. Later, in *Jacobowsky and the Colonel* (1944) and *The Magnificent Yankee* (1946; as Justice Oliver Wendell Holmes). Last N.Y. appearance as King Lear, 1950.

294

295

296

294. LUCILE WATSON (1879–1962; born in Canada). Debut, 1900, Ottawa; N.Y., 1902. Major plays included: *The City* (1909); the world premiere of *Heartbreak House* (1920); *Pride and Prejudice* (1935); *Yes, My Darling Daughter* (1937); *Watch on the Rhine* (1941); and *Ring Round the Moon* (1950; her last in N.Y.). **295. BLANCHE YURKA** (actually, Jurka; 1893–1974; born in Bohemia). Studied opera; was super in first Metropolitan Opera *Parsifal*, 1905. Broadway debut, 1907, as understudy in *The Warrens of Virginia*; roles from 1909. John Barrymore's Gertrude in his great *Hamlet* (1922). In *Man and the Masses* (1924) and *Goat Song* (1926) for the Theatre Guild. Hit in *The Squall* (1926). Much Ibsen, Shakespeare, Greek drama. In *Lucrece* (1932). Succeeded Edith Evans as Nurse to Cornell's Juliet, N.Y., 1935. One-woman shows, 1936–38 (also, 1963). Last N.Y. play, 1970. **296. JOSEPHINE HULL** (née Sherwood; 1886–1957; was married to Shelley Hull, brother of Henry Hull, no. 259). Debut at the Castle Square, Boston, 1905. Retirement, 1919–22, after husband's death. Regular work in N.Y., 1923–53, in such plays as: *Fata Morgana* (1924); *Craig's Wife* (1925); *You Can't Take It with You* (1936); *Arsenic and Old Lace* (1941); *Harvey* (1944); and *The Solid Gold Cadillac* (1953).

297

298

299

300

301

302

297. PERCY WARAM (ca. 1881–1961; born in England). Debut, 1899, with Ben Greet. N.Y., 1902. Magnificent career included: Horatio in Basil Sydney's modern-dress *Hamlet* (1925); *Mary of Scotland* (1933); *Pride and Prejudice* (1935); *The Merchant of Yonkers* (1938); tour and N.Y. takeover in *Life with Father* (1941); *The Late George Apley* (1944); *Another Part of the Forest* (1946); Wolsey in *Anne of the Thousand Days* (1948); and *The Chalk Garden* (1955). Last N.Y. play, 1957. **298. HOWARD LINDSAY** (1889–1968; married Dorothy Stickney, 1927). Principally a preeminent playwright, producer and director, he was also an actor. Debut, 1909, in tour of *Polly of the Circus*. With Margaret Anglin, 1913–18 (N.Y. debut, 1914). N.Y. acting credits included (* = wrote or co-authored): *Dulcy* (1921; he also directed); *Life with Father* (1939;*; greatest hit; long, long run); *Life with Mother* (1948;*); *Remains to Be Seen* (1951;*); and *One Bright Day* (1952; his last in N.Y.). **299. DOROTHY STICKNEY** (born 1900; widow of no. 298). Debut, 1921, in North Dakota; N.Y., 1926, in *The Squall*. Major N.Y. plays: *Chicago* (1926); *The Front Page* (1928); *On Borrowed Time* (1938); *Life with Father* (1939; also in 1967 revival); *Life with Mother* (1948) and *Kind Sir* (1952). In N.Y. in 1960 and 1964 with one-woman show. Latest N.Y. appearance, 1973. **300. JESSIE ROYCE LANDIS** (née Medbury; 1904–1972). Debut, 1924,

Chicago; N.Y., 1926. Also an accomplished singer, she had the lead in the out-of-town tryout of *The New Moon* in 1928. In N.Y., in many revivals, and in: *Love's Old Sweet Song* (1940); *Kiss and Tell* (1943); and *Roar Like a Dove* (1964). Successful London appearances, 1950/1, especially in the musical version of *And So to Bed* (1951). Special matinees, N.Y., 1967. **301. BETTY FIELD** (1918–1973; married, 1942–55, to playwright Elmer Rice). Debut, 1933, Stockbridge, Mass.; London, 1934; N.Y., same year, in *Page Miss Glory*. Later, in *Room Service* (1937) and *What a Life* (1939; the play in which the character Henry Aldrich first appeared). Succeeded Margaret Sullavan in *The Voice of the Turtle*, 1944. In *Dream Girl* (1945). Succeeded Jessica Tandy in *The Fourposter*, 1952. In national company of *The Waltz of the Toreadors*, 1957/8; other tours and revivals. Two N.Y. plays, 1971. **302. MARGARET SULLAVAN** (1911–1960; was married to Henry Fonda and to film director William Wyler). Worked with the Baltimore University Players, E. E. Clive's stock company in Boston, and the University Players on Cape Cod (see no. 287) before her N.Y. debut in 1931. Main N.Y. plays: *Stage Door* (1936); (after 7 years in Hollywood) *The Voice of the Turtle* (1943); *The Deep Blue Sea* (1952); *Sabrina Fair* (1953); and *Janus* (1955). Successful in films from 1933. Was touring in a pre-Broadway tryout at the time of her death.

117

303

303. **MILDRED NATWICK** (born 1908). Debut, 1929, Baltimore. With University Players on Cape Cod (see no. 287). N.Y. debut, 1932. In: *End of Summer* (1936); *Blithe Spirit* (1941; as Mme. Arcati); *The Grass Harp* (1952); *The Waltz of the Toreadors* (1957); and *Barefoot in the Park* (1963). Latest N.Y. appearance, 1979. 304. **SHIRLEY BOOTH** (real name, Thelma Booth Ford; born 1907). Began in stock, Hartford, ca. 1920; N.Y. debut, 1925. Biggest successes: *Three Men on a Horse* (1935); *The Philadelphia Story* (1939); *My Sister Eileen* (1940); *Tomorrow the World* (1943); *Goodbye, My Fancy* (1948; Tony award); *Come Back, Little Sheba* (1950; second Tony); the musical *A Tree Grows in Brooklyn* (1951); *The Time of the Cuckoo* (1952; third Tony); and the musicals *By the Beautiful Sea* (1954) and *Juno* (1959). Latest N.Y. play, 1970; play in San Francisco, 1971. Oscar, 1952, for film version of *Come Back, Little Sheba*. On radio in *Duffy's Tavern*. On TV in *Hazel* (has received Emmy award).

304

305. MILDRED Dorothy **DUNNOCK** (born 1906). N.Y. debut, 1932. In: *The Eternal Road* (1937); *The Corn Is Green* (1940); *Foolish Notion* (1945); *Lute Song* and *Another Part of the Forest* (both 1946); *Death of a Salesman* (1949; as Linda Loman); *Cat on a Hot Tin Roof* (1955). Many classic revivals. Latest N.Y. appearance, 1977. At Stratford, Conn., 1956; at Spoleto Festival, 1962 and 1963. **306. ETHEL WATERS** (1896–1977). One of our greatest popular singers (she began in vaudeville in 1917) and a delight in many Broadway musicals between 1927 and 1953 (e.g., *As Thousands Cheer*, 1933; *At Home Abroad*, 1935; *Cabin in the Sky*, 1940), she also belongs in any elite gathering of nonmusical actresses for her work in *Mamba's Daughters* (1938) and *The Member of the Wedding* (1950; also in revival out of N.Y., 1964). Films, 1929–59. In her last years, sang at religious rallies.

307

308

307. SIR LAURENCE OLIVIER (knighted 1947; English; born 1907; married, 1930–40, to actress Jill Esmond; 1940–60, to Vivien Leigh; from 1961, to Joan Plowright). Debut, London, 1924. With Birmingham Repertory Company, 1926–28. The very first Captain Stanhope in *Journey's End*, London, 1928. From the mid-1930s, concentrated on Shakespeare at the Old Vic and elsewhere, but has done all kinds of classic and modern roles in astonishing career. Director of the Chichester Festival, 1961. Director of the National Theatre, 1963–73. His N.Y. appearances, between 1929 and 1960, included: *Private Lives* (1931; in the original London cast, 1930); *The Green Bay Tree* (1933); *No Time for Comedy* (1939); *The Entertainer* (1958); and *Becket* (1960); as well as Shakespeare and Shaw. Oscar for performance in his own film of *Hamlet* (1948). **308. JUDITH EVELYN** (Judith Evelyn Allen; 1913–1967). Debut, 1928, Winnipeg; several years in Canada. London, 1938. In Hollywood, 1941, in the U.S. premiere of *Gaslight*, which came to N.Y. with her (her debut there) as *Angel Street* in the same year. Other great N.Y. role: *The Shrike* (1952). Last N.Y. play, 1960. At the Guthrie Theatre, Minneapolis, 1963. **309.** Jessica Tandy and Hume Cronyn (married since 1942; she had been married, from 1932, to Jack Hawkins). **JESSICA**

TANDY (born 1909 in England). Debut, 1927; at Birmingham Rep, 1928; London, 1929. Ophelia in Gielgud's first major *Hamlet*, 1934. At Old Vic, 1937 and 1940. In creations of *French Without Tears* (1936) and *Time and the Conways* (1938). In the latter play (same year), she made her N.Y. debut. In *Geneva* (1940). Appearance in one-acters by Tennessee Williams in Los Angeles, 1946, led to the role of her lifetime: Blanche DuBois in *A Streetcar Named Desire* (1947; Tony award). Later (* = with Hume Cronyn): *The Fourposter* (1951;*); *The Man in the Dog Suit* (1957; N.Y., 1958;*); *Five Finger Exercise* (1959); *The Physicists* (1964;*); *A Delicate Balance* (1966;*); *The Gin Game* (1977;*; her second Tony); *Foxfire* (1982;*). **HUME CRONYN** (born 1911 in Canada). In student plays at McGill, 1930/1; professional debut in Washington, D.C., stock, 1931; N.Y., 1934. In *High Tor* (1937). Much work, as director as well as actor, at Skowhegan, in army camps, in Los Angeles, on tours, etc. Instrumental in founding of off-Broadway Phoenix Theatre, N.Y., 1953, and of Guthrie Theatre, Minneapolis, 1963. For plays with Jessica Tandy, see above. Other N.Y. plays with him: *Big Fish, Little Fish* (1961); Richard Burton's *Hamlet* (1964; as Polonius; Tony award). Both of them have appeared extensively in regional theater all around the country.

311

310

312

310. MARLON BRANDO (Jr.; born 1924). Before his fabulous film career began in 1950 (Oscar, 1954, for *On the Waterfront*), he was an important stage actor. Debut, 1944, N.Y.; that year, in *I Remember Mama*. In 1946, in: *Truckline Café*; a revival of *Candida*; and *A Flag Is Born*. Sensation in 1947 as Stanley Kowalski in *A Streetcar Named Desire*. **311. CANADA LEE** (real name, Leonard Lionel Cornelius Canegata; 1907–1952). Debut, 1928, N.Y. In second season of the play *Stevedore* (1934). Banquo in the Negro People's Theatre *Macbeth* (1936). In the Federal Theatre *Haiti* (1938). Later plays included: *Mamba's Daughters* (1939); *Native Son* (1941); *Anna Lucasta* (1944); *The Tempest* (1945; as Caliban); and *On Whitman Avenue* (1946). Last N.Y. play, 1948. **312. WILLIAM** Leroy **PRINCE** (born 1913). N.Y. debut, 1937, in walk-on part in *The Eternal Road*. A page in the Maurice Evans *Hamlet* (1938); also in Evans' *Henry IV, Part I* (1939). Later, in: *Guest in the House* and *The Eve of St. Mark* (both 1942); *I Am a Camera* (1951); *The Ballad of the Sad Café* (1963); and Albee's *The Man Who Had Three Arms* (1983).

313. JOSÉ Vicente **FERRER** (born 1912 in Puerto Rico; married, 1938–48, to Uta Hagen, no. 318; from 1953, to Rosemary Clooney). Debut, 1934, on a Long Island showboat; Broadway, 1935. In: *Brother Rat* (1936); *Mamba's Daughters* and *Key Largo* (both 1939); a revival of *Charley's Aunt* (1940; again, 1953); the Robeson *Othello* (1943; as Iago); a revival of *Cyrano de Bergerac* (1946; Tony award; revived again, 1953). In 1948, as general director of the N.Y. City Theatre Company, in outstanding productions of *Volpone, The Alchemist* and other classics. Same year, on Broadway, in *The Silver Whistle*. In 1952, in *The Shrike* (his second Tony; also directed). Operatic debut, 1960, Santa Fe. Between 1966 and 1968, tours in *The Man of La Mancha*, with several weeks in N.Y. Latest N.Y., 1978, succeeding Ellis Rabb in *A Life in the Theater* (off-Broadway). In a 1982 film. Oscar for the 1950 film version of *Cyrano*. **314.** George **ORSON WELLES** (born 1915). Acted at age 9. Professional debut at the Dublin Gate Theatre, 1931. On Katharine Cornell's tour, 1933/4; Broadway debut, 1934, as Tybalt in her *Romeo and Juliet*. Directed for the Federal Theatre Project in N.Y., 1936/7; acted in *Dr. Faustus* (1937). Later in 1937, founded the Mercury Theatre in N.Y. with John Houseman; acted in *Julius Caesar* (1937) among other Mercury productions. Meanwhile, important radio work (especially *The War of the Worlds*, 1938). From 1940, chiefly in the film world. Latest Broadway acting, 1946. On stage in Paris, 1950; in London, 1951 and 1955. Latest time in N.Y., 1956, as Lear at the City Center. Latest of all, 1960, in Dublin. TV commercials in 1980s.

315

316

317

315. FRANK FAY (1897–1961; married in 1930s to Barbara Stanwyck). Debut, 1901; N.Y., 1903. Many years in vaudeville. Adult career in N.Y. from 1918, chiefly in lowdown musicals: *Frank Fay's Fables* (1922); *Delmar's Revels* (1927). In 1933, put together the show *Tattle Tales* in California and brought it to N.Y. Catapulted to enduring fame as Elwood P. Dowd in *Harvey* (1944; role in photo), one of the classic Broadway performances (and his last). In a San Francisco show, 1950. **316. RICHARD WARING** (Richard Waring Stephens; born 1912 in England). Apprentice in Eva Le Gallienne's Civic Repertory Company, 1930; with her several years (original White Rabbit in *Alice in Wonderland*, 1932); appeared with her in 1939 in a Frank Fay show.

Fame, 1940, in *The Corn Is Green*, with Ethel Barrymore. In *Truckline Café*, 1946. Once again associated with Le Gallienne in the American Repertory Theatre, 1946/7. In classic revivals off-Broadway, 1953–64. At Stratford, Conn., 1957–62. Latest N.Y. play, 1968. **317. TOM EWELL** (real name, Yewell Tompkins; born 1908). Debut, 1928, in Madison, Wis.; N.Y., 1934, in *They Shall Not Die*. Also in: *Ethan Frome* and *Stage Door* (both 1936); *The Merchant of Yonkers* (1938); *Family Portrait* (1939); *John Loves Mary* (1947); *The Seven Year Itch* (1952; his biggest hit; Tony award); *The Tunnel of Love* (1957); and *The Thurber Carnival* (1960). Latest N.Y. play, 1965. Extensive touring. Acted in Los Angeles in the 1979/80 season.

318

318. Uta Hagen and Paul Kelly in *The Country Girl*, 1950. **UTA** Thyra **HAGEN** (born 1919 in Germany; married, 1938–48, to José Ferrer, no. 313; from 1951, to Herbert Berghof). College plays in Wisconsin, mid-1930s. N.Y. debut, 1938, in *The Seagull*, with the Lunts. Later, in *Key Largo* (1939) and the Robeson *Othello* (1943; as Desdemona; she had toured in that role for the Theatre Guild in 1942). Succeeded Jessica Tandy in *A Streetcar Named Desire*, 1948, and toured in it into 1949. Back in N.Y.: *The Country Girl* (1950; Tony award); a revival of *Saint Joan* (1951); *Any Language* (1952); *Island of Goats* (1955); *The Good Woman of Setzuan* (1956); and *Who's Afraid of Virginia Woolf?* (1962; her second Tony; also in the London cast, 1964). Latest N.Y. play, 1980. On TV in 1982. Teacher of acting at her own N.Y. school (with Berghof). **PAUL KELLY** (1899–1956). Debut at 8. N.Y. plays included: *Seventeen* and *Penrod* (both 1918); *Chains* (1923; with Helen Gahagan); and *The Nine-Fifteen Revue* (1930; musical). Away from N.Y. stage, 1932–45. Later, in *Command Decision* (1947) and *The Country Girl* (1950; his last in N.Y.). **319.** Frank **KENT SMITH** (born 1907). Debut, 1917, N.Y. Member of the University Players in Cape Cod in the late 1920s (see no. 287). Adult N.Y. career from 1932. In: *Dodsworth* (1934); two 1936 Cornell productions, *Saint Joan* and *The Wingless Victory*; *The Star Wagon* (1937); *Antony and Cleopatra* (1947; again with Cornell); *The Wisteria Trees* (1950); and *The Autumn Garden* (1951). Latest N.Y. play, 1956. In Los Angeles, 1977. **320. RICHARD** Baker **WHORF** (1906–1966). Debut, 1921, in Boston stock; N.Y., 1927. Member of Theatre Guild, 1935 ff. With the Lunts in: *Idiot's Delight* (1936); *Amphitryon 38* (1937); and *There Shall Be No Night* (1940; also did the sets). Later, in *A Season in the Sun* (1950) and *The Fifth Season* (1953; his last in N.Y.). Active 1960. Also important as director. **321. ELISABETH BERGNER** (born 1897 in Poland). Debut, 1915, in Innsbruck (Austria). Vast German-speaking career, including work with Reinhardt; international fame in *Saint Joan*, 1924. English-language debut, 1933, London, in *Escape Me Never*; N.Y. debut in same play, 1935. In London, 1936, in title role of Barrie's last play, *The Boy David* (written for her). Later N.Y. appearances: *The Two Mrs. Carrolls* (1943); a revival of *The Duchess of Malfi* (1946); and *The Cup of Trembling* (1948). In New Haven, 1961. Back to Germany from the 1960s (in London, 1973). Began directing in Germany, 1970. Films and TV there, ca. 1980.

322. John **ARTHUR KENNEDY** (born 1914). Debut, 1934, with Group Theatre in N.Y., in *Merrily We Roll Along*, billed as John Kennedy (during 1939, "John" changed to "J. Arthur"; in 1940, to "Arthur"). In Maurice Evans' *Richard II* (1937) and *Henry IV, Part I* (1939). From 1947, an Arthur Miller specialist; in: *All My Sons* (1947); *Death of a Salesman* (1949; Tony award); and *The Price* (1968; his latest in N.Y.). **323. RALPH BELLAMY** (born 1904). Debut in the Midwest, early 1920s. Stock in various cities, at times with his own company, to 1930. N.Y. debut, 1929. Chief N.Y. plays: *Tomorrow the World* (1943); *State of the Union* (1945); *Detective Story* (1949); and *Sunrise at Campobello* (1958; role in photo; Tony award; his latest in N.Y.). Very popular in films up to at least 1983.

324

325

324. BARBARA BEL GEDDES (born 1922; daughter of eminent theatrical and industrial designer Norman Bel Geddes). Debut, 1940, in Connecticut stock; N.Y., 1941. In: *Deep Are the Roots* (1945); *Burning Bright* (1950); *The Moon Is Blue* (1951); *The Living Room* (1954); *Cat on a Hot Tin Roof* (1955); *The Sleeping Prince* (1956); and *Mary, Mary* (1961). Latest N.Y. play, 1973. In Chicago, 1977. TV in 1980s. **325. DAVID WAYNE** (real name, Wayne James McMeekan; born 1914). Debut in Shakespeare at the 1936 Cleveland Exposition; N.Y., 1938. Chief N.Y. credits: *Finian's Rainbow* (1947; as the leprechaun; Tony award); *Mister Roberts* (1948; as Ensign Pulver); *The Teahouse of the August Moon* (1953; second Tony); a revival of *Too True to Be Good* (1963); and *After the Fall* (1964). Latest N.Y. play, 1965. Active 1972.

326. JULIE (Julia Ann) **HARRIS** (born 1925). School plays at age 14; N.Y., 1945. Bit parts in N.Y. with Old Vic (1946); the American Repertory Theatre (1946/7); and Michael Redgrave's *Macbeth* (1948; as one of the witches). Success in *The Member of the Wedding* (1950; role in photo); then in: *I Am a Camera* (1951), *The Lark* (1955) and *A Shot in the Dark* (1961). Continuous N.Y. career has included two Tony-winning performances: *The Last of Mrs. Lincoln* (1972) and *The Belle of Amherst* (1976). Latest N.Y. play, 1980. **327. KIM HUNTER** (real name, Janet Cole; born 1922). Debut, 1939, in a Florida club; N.Y., 1947, as Stella Kowalski in *A Streetcar Named Desire*. Later, in: *Darkness at Noon* (1951); *The Chase* (1952); and *The Tender Trap* (1954). She has played many top roles in other cities. Latest N.Y. play, 1981. At Stratford, Conn., 1961. Oscar, 1951, for film version of *Streetcar*. **328. BEATRICE** Whitney **STRAIGHT** (born 1918). Debut, 1935, N.Y. Outstanding in *The Innocents* (1950) and *The Crucible* (1953; Tony award). Latest N.Y. appearance, 1980. A founder of Theatre, Inc., which brought the Old Vic to N.Y. for the first time (1946).

327

328

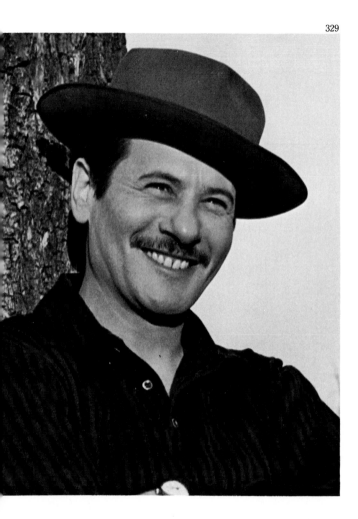

329. ELI WALLACH (born 1915; married, from 1948, to Anne Jackson). Acted in a Brooklyn club, 1930; Broadway, 1945. In American Repertory Theatre, 1946/7; charter member of Actors' Studio, 1947. In: *The Rose Tattoo* (1951; Tony); *Camino Real* (1953); *The Cold Wind and the Warm* (1958); and *Rhinoceros* (1961; with Anne Jackson). Off-Broadway with her, 1963, in the double bill *The Typists* and *The Tiger*; again with her in *Luv* (1964). Numerous N.Y. appearances separately or with his wife, the latest being in 1982 (together). **330. ANNE** (Anna June) **JACKSON** (born 1926). Debut, 1944, in a tour of *The Cherry Orchard* (N.Y., 1945). In American Repertory Theatre, 1946/7. Important N.Y. plays: *Summer and Smoke* (1948); *Oh Men! Oh Women!* (1953); *The Middle of the Night* (1956); *Brecht on Brecht* (1962). Latest N.Y. play without her husband Eli Wallach, 1977; for her appearances along with him, see no. 329. **331. E. G. MARSHALL** (born 1910). Debut, 1933, in touring repertory. N.Y., 1938, in *Prologue to Glory*. Also in: *The Skin of Our Teeth* (1942); *Jacobowsky and the Colonel* (1944); *The Iceman Cometh* (1946); *The Crucible* (1953); *Red Roses for Me* (1955); *Waiting for Godot* (1956); and *The Gang's All Here* (1959). Latest N.Y. appearance, 1980. Vast amount of TV work; numerous films.

Notes on the Photographs

The numbers are those of the illustrations.

Frontispiece: From Skinner's second film version of *Kismet*, 1930 (First National); photo by Elmer Fryer. **1:** After a daguerreotype of 1850. **2:** Photo by Sarony, N.Y. **4:** In the role of Jack Cade. **10:** As Rip Van Winkle. **13 & 14:** Photos by Caldesi, Blanford & Co., London. **15:** Photo by C. D. Mosher, Chicago. **16:** Photo by Warren, Boston. **18:** Photo by C. F. Conly (successor to Warren), Boston. **19:** Photo by Sarony, N.Y. **21:** Photo by Sarony, N.Y. In the title role of *Mary Warner.* **22:** Photo by J. F. Ryder, Cleveland; signed 1882. **24:** Photo by Sarony, N.Y. **25:** Photo by Chas. L. Ritzmann, N.Y. **26:** Photo by Sarony, N.Y. In the title role of *Rose Michel.* **27:** Photo ca. 1899. **28:** As Louise in *The Two Orphans.* **29:** Photo by Sarony, N.Y. As Eliot Gray in *Rosedale.* **30:** Photo by Sarony, N.Y. As Lord Dundreary in *Our American Cousin.* **32:** Photo by Houseworth & Co., San Francisco; signed 1877. **33:** Photo by C. F. Conly, Boston. **34:** Photo by Sarony, N.Y. As Picard in *The Two Orphans.* **35:** Photo by Julius Ulke, Washington, D.C., 1875. **36:** Photo by B. F. Falk, N.Y.; signed 1883. **37:** Figaro-Programme photo, London. **38:** Photo by Sarony, N.Y., ca. 1899. **39:** Photo by Scholl, Philadelphia. **40:** Photo by Sarony, N.Y. **42:** Photo by Window & Grove, London; signed 1910. **43:** Photo by Window & Grove, London. **45:** Photo by F. N. Tomlinson, Detroit. **46:** Photo by Morrison, Chicago. **47:** Photo by B. F. Falk, N.Y. **48:** Photo by Pach Bros., N.Y. **49:** Photo by Sarony, N.Y. **50:** Photo by Sarony, N.Y., 1891. As Lady Teazle in *The School for Scandal.* **52:** Photo by Scholl, Philadelphia; signed 1879. **55:** Photo by Elmer Chickering, Boston. **57:** Photo ca. 1899. **58:** In the title role of the film *The Count of Monte Cristo,* 1913 (Famous Players). **59:** Photo by Hall, N.Y. In the vaudeville sketch *The Phantom Highwayman,* 1907. **60:** In the title role of *Griffith Davenport.* **61:** Photo by Frank C. Bangs, ca. 1910. **62:** Photo by S. L. Stein. **63:** Photo by B. F. Falk, N.Y. **64:** Photo ca. 1904. **65:** Photo by Sarony, N.Y.; signed 1894. **66:** Photo by White, N.Y. **67:** Photo by Otto Sarony Co., N.Y. **68:** In the play *Sapho.* **70:** Photo by Elmer Chickering, Boston. **71:** Photo by Otto Sarony Co., N.Y. In the title role of *Peter Pan.* **72:** Photo ca. 1899. **73:** In a Fox film, 1916. **74:** MGM photo. **75:** In *Kick In,* 1914. **76:** Photo by White, N.Y., with a release by Charles Frohman. **77:** Photo by Sarony, N.Y. **78:** Photo by White, N.Y., ca. 1917. **79:** Photo by Burr McIntosh Studio, N.Y. In *A Gentleman of France.* **80:** Photo by Moffett, Chicago, 1915. **81:** Photo by Otto Sarony Co., N.Y. In the title role of *The Girl of the Golden West.* **83:** Photo ca. 1899. **84:** Photo by Strauss-Peyton, Kansas City. In *The Great Divide.* **86:** Photo by Pach, N.Y. **87:** Photo ca. 1899. **88:** Photo by Pach Bros., N.Y. **89:** Photo by Otto Sarony Co., N.Y. In *Man and Superman.* **90:** Photo by Window & Grove, London; signed 1907. Perhaps as Portia in *The Merchant of Venice.* **91:** Photo by B. F. Falk, N.Y. **92:** Photo by Aimé Dupont, N.Y.; signed 1900. **93:** Photo signed 1907. As Imogen in *Cymbeline.* **94:** Photo by Bates & Muhr, Denver; signed 1883. **95:** In the film *A Tale of Two Cities,* 1917 (Fox). **96:** Photo by Otto Sarony Co., N.Y., ca. 1906. **97:** Photo by Moffett, Chicago, ca. 1912. **98:** Photo by Frank C. Bangs, N.Y. In *The Call of the Cricket,* 1910. **99:** Photo by Morrison, Chicago. **100:** Photo by Schloss, N.Y. **101:** Photo by White, N.Y., 1910. **102:** Photo by Sarony, N.Y. **103:** Photo by Moffett, Chicago, ca. 1911. **104:** Photo by Elmer Chickering, Boston. **105:** Ca. 1933. **106:** In *Sinners,* 1915. **109:** Photo ca. 1924. **110:** Photo by Sarony, N.Y., ca. 1909. **111:** Photo by Sarony, N.Y. In *Just a Wife,* 1910. **112:** Photo by White, N.Y., ca. 1912. **113:** Photo ca. 1906. **114:** Photo by Sands & Brady, Providence. **115:** Photo by White, N.Y., 1910. **116:** Photo by Moffett, Chicago, ca. 1912. **117:** Photo by Falk Studios, Melbourne & Sydney. In *A Gentleman of France.* **118:** Photo by White, N.Y. In *The Prince Chap.* **120:** In the title role of the film *Oliver Twist,* 1916 (Lasky Feature Play Co.). **121:** Photo by Campbell, ca. 1919. **122:** Photo by White, N.Y. In the 1915 revival of *The New York Idea.* **123:** Photo by Pinchot Studios, ca. 1928. **124:** In *The Duchess of Dantzic* (London, 1903; N.Y., 1905). **126:** Photo by C. Smith Gardner; signed 1918. **127:** In *Grounds for Divorce,* 1924. **128:** Photo accompanied by a quotation from *The Sign of the Cross.* **129:** Photo signed 1907. **130:** In *The Son-Daughter.* **131:** Photo by Parry (Pittsburgh?). **132:** Photo 1915. **133:** Photo ca. 1927. **134:** Photo ca. 1938 in Hollywood. **137:** In the film *When the Clouds Roll By,* 1919 (Douglas Fairbanks Pictures Corp.). **138:** Photo ca. 1924. **139:** Photo by White, N.Y. **140:** Photo by C. Smith Gardner, ca. 1924. **141:** Photo by Hall-Stearn, ca. 1925. **142:** Photo by White, N.Y. In *The Pigeon.* **143:** Photo by White, N.Y. In *As a Man Thinks,* 1911. **144:** Photo by Sarony, N.Y., ca. 1911. **145:** Photo by Maurice Goldberg, ca. 1925. **146:** In *Dr. Syn,* 1937 (Gaumont-British), Arliss' last film. **148:** In *Hell-Bent fer Heaven,* 1924. **149:** MGM photo, 1946. **150:** Photo by White, N.Y. In *Major Pendennis,* 1916. **152:** In *The Havoc,* 1911. **153:** Photo by White, N.Y. In *He Comes Up Smiling,* 1914. **154:** Photo by Matzene, Chicago, ca. 1911. **155:** Photo ca. 1906. **156:** In *The Great Adventure,* 1913. **157:** In *Septimus,* 1909. **159:** Photo by White, N.Y., 1917. **160:** Photo by Sarony, N.Y. In *Cheating Cheaters,* 1916. **161:** Photo by the Tonnele Co. **162:** Photo signed 1919. **163:** As Romeo, 1919. **164:** In *Another Way Out,* 1916. **165:** Photo 1917. **166:** Photo by Underwood & Underwood, 1917. **167:** Photo by White, N.Y.; signed 1913. **168 & 169:** Photos ca. 1930. **170:** Photo by Hutchinson, ca. 1919. **172:** Photo by Hartsook, San Francisco & Los Angeles. **173:** Photo ca. 1930. **174:** Photo by Maurice Goldberg, ca. 1924. **175:** Photo by Alfred Cheney Johnston. As Portia in *The Merchant of Venice,* 1922. **176:** Signed by the photographer, Strauss-Peyton, Kansas City, 1918. **177:** In *The Little Foxes,* 1939. **178:** Photo by Francis Bruguière. In the title role of *The Emperor Jones.* **179:** Photo by Lucas & Monroe, N.Y. In the title role of *John Henry,* 1940. **180:** Photo by Vandamm, N.Y. In *Porgy,* 1927. **181:** Photo by Hommel, ca. 1930. **182:** Photo ca. 1930. **183:** In the film *The Sin Ship,* 1931 (RKO Radio). **185:** Photo by Pinchot, ca. 1928. **186:** Photo by Nickolas Muray, N.Y., ca. 1928. **187:** Photo by Victor Georg, ca. 1924. **188:** Photo by Nicholas Haz. In the title role of *Major Barbara,* 1928. **189:** Photo by Nicholas Haz, ca. 1927. **190:** Photo by Vandamm Studios, N.Y., ca. 1928. **191:** MGM photo, 1933. **192:** Photo from mid-1920s. **193:** Photo by Charles Synder. As Chico in *Seventh Heaven.* **195:** Photo by Vandamm, N.Y., ca. 1926. **196:** Photo by Vandamm, N.Y., ca. 1926. Wearing a blonde wig for *Gentlemen Prefer Blondes.* **197:** In *Sun-Up.* **198:** Photo ca. 1945. **200:** In the film *Remodeling Her Husband,* 1920 (New Art Film Co.). **201:** Photo by Mishkin, N.Y. **202:** In the film *Sins of Man,* 1936 (20th Century-Fox). **203:** In the film *Queen Christina,* 1934 (MGM). **204:** In Olivier's film version of *Hamlet,* 1948 (Two Cities). **206:**

Photo by A. L. Schafer for Columbia Pictures. **208:** As Miss Havisham in the film *Great Expectations*, 1934 (Universal). **209:** Photo by White, N.Y. In *Some Baby!*, 1915. **211:** Photo by Vandamm, N.Y., ca. 1925. **213:** Photo by Vandamm, N.Y., ca. 1930. **214:** Photo by Vandamm, N.Y. **215:** Photo by Hal Phyfe, N.Y., ca. 1928. **216:** Associated Press photo. In *The Taming of the Shrew*, 1935. **217:** In the film *Viva Villa!*, 1934 (MGM). **218:** In the film *Crime Without Passion*, 1934 (Paramount). **219:** Photo ca. 1930. **220:** Photo by Vandamm, N.Y. In *The Front Page*, 1928. **221:** In the film *Shadow of a Doubt*, 1943 (Universal). **222:** In the title role of the film *She*, 1935 (RKO Radio). **223:** In the film *Tiger Shark*, 1932 (Warner Bros.) **224:** Photo by Nickolas Muray, ca. 1930. As the secretary in her monodrama *Three Women and Mr. Clifford*. **226:** In the film *The Man Who Could Work Miracles*, 1936 (London Films). **227:** Photo by Maurice Goldberg. In *The Living Corpse*, 1929. **228:** In *Call It a Day*, 1936. **229:** Photo 1934. **230:** In the film *Dracula*, 1931 (Universal). **231:** Photo by White, N.Y., ca. 1930. **232:** In the film *The Devil's Lottery*, 1932 (Fox). **233:** In the film *Moulin Rouge*, 1934 (20th Century-Fox). **234:** Photo ca. 1929. **235:** MGM photo, probably 1935. **236:** In the film *Intermezzo*, 1939 (United Artists). **237:** In the film *The Vagabond King*, 1930 (Paramount). **238:** In the film *Sweet Adeline*, 1934 (Warner Bros.). **240:** Paramount Pictures photo, 1935. **241:** In the film *Four Sons*, 1940 (20th Century-Fox). **242:** Universal-International Pictures photo, 1947. **243:** In the film *Alice Adams*, 1935 (RKO Radio). **244:** In the film *Nothing But the Truth*, 1941 (Paramount). **245:** MGM photo, 1932/3 period. **247:** Photo by White, N.Y. In *Counsellor-at-Law*, 1931. **248:** Photo by Talbot, N.Y. In *When We Are Married*, 1939. **249:** Photo by Hartsook, San Francisco & Los Angeles. In *Seven Chances*, 1916. **250:** NBC photo, 1939. **251:** Photo by Vandamm, N.Y. In *Love for Love*, 1940. **252:** Photo by Doris Ulmann, N.Y. As Helena in *Uncle Vanya*, 1930. **253:** In the 1930 London revival of *The Devil's Disciple*. **254:** Photo by Vandamm, N.Y. In *The Time of Your Life*. **255:** Photo by Count Jean de Strelecki. **256:** Photo by Zinn Arthur, Hollywood. In *The Lovers*, 1956. **257:** In the film *My Girl Tisa*, 1948 (Warner Bros.). **258:** In the film *The Wake of the Red Witch*, 1948 (Republic). **259:** Photo by Vandamm, N.Y. In *The Masque of Kings*, 1937. **260:** Photo by Alex Kahle. In the film *Abe Lincoln in Illinois*, 1940 (RKO Radio). **261:** Photo by Eugene Robert Richee (?). In the film *Second Chorus*, 1941 (Paramount). **262:** Photo by Vandamm, N.Y. In *Love for Love*, 1940. **263:** In the title role of *Hamlet*, 1936 (N.Y.). **265:** MGM photo, probably 1939. **266:** NBC-TV photo. In the Hallmark Hall of Fame telecast of *Macbeth*, 1954. **267:** Photo by Vandamm, N.Y. In *Romeo and Juliet*, 1934. Inscribed by Cornell to Jo Mielziner,

designer of the production. **268:** Photo by Talbot, N.Y., ca. 1946. **269:** In *The Little Foxes*, 1939. **270:** Fox photo, ca. 1935. **271:** Photo ca. 1959. **272:** Photo by Hartsook, San Francisco & Los Angeles, ca. 1928. **273:** Photo ca. 1947. **274:** Photo ca. 1949. **275:** Photo ca. 1944. **276:** Photo by Vandamm, N.Y. In *Kindred*, 1939. **277:** Photo by Alfredo Valente, in connection with *On Borrowed Time*, 1938. **278:** In the film *Framed*, 1940 (Universal). **279:** In the film *Love Me or Leave Me*, 1955 (MGM). **280:** In the film *Spy Ring*, 1938 (Universal). **281:** In the film *Charlie Chan's Murder Cruise*, 1940 (20th Century-Fox). **282:** In the film *Glamour Boy*, 1941 (Paramount). **283:** Photo by Alfredo Valente. In *The Shoemaker's Holiday*. **284:** Photo by Talmage Morrison for Paramount, 1939. **285:** Columbia Pictures photo. **286:** In the film *Intermezzo*, 1939 (United Artists). **287:** Photo by Pat Clark. In the film *No Time for Sergeants*, 1958 (Warner Bros.). **289:** Photo by Kenneth Alexander for Goldwyn Pictures, 1930. **290:** NBC photo. In the title role of *Victoria Regina*, 1935. **291:** In the film *Boomerang*, 1947 (20th Century-Fox). **292:** ABC-TV photo, 1973. In the series *The Streets of San Francisco*. **293:** In the film *The Bridge of San Luis Rey*, 1943 (United Artists). **294:** In the film *Watch on the Rhine*, 1943 (Warner Bros.). **295:** In the film *Queen of the Mob*, 1940 (Paramount). **296:** In the film version of *Harvey*, 1950 (Universal-International). **297:** In the film version of *The Late George Apley*, 1947 (20th Century-Fox). **299:** Photo by Vandamm, N.Y. **300:** In the film *It Happens Every Spring*, 1949 (20th Century-Fox). **301:** Photo ca. 1955. **303:** In the film *The Late George Apley*, 1947 (20th Century-Fox). **304:** Photo by Alfredo Valente. In *Love Me Long*, 1949. **305:** In the film *Butterfield 8*, 1960 (MGM). **306:** Photo by Alfredo Valente. **307:** In the title role of his film *Hamlet*, 1948 (Two Cities). **308:** Photo by Talbot, N.Y., ca. 1942. **309:** Photo by Clarence S. Bull for MGM, 1944. **311:** Photo ca. 1945. **312:** Photo by Coburn, Jr., for Columbia Pictures, 1956. **313:** MGM photo, probably 1950. **315:** Photo by Vandamm, N.Y. In *Harvey*. **316:** In the film *Mr. Skeffington*, 1944 (Warner Bros.). **317:** 20th Century-Fox photo, 1956. **318:** In *The Country Girl*, 1950. **315:** In the film *Paula*, 1952 (Columbia). **320:** In the film *Midnight*, 1934 (Universal). **321:** Photo by Trude Geiringer, 1927. **322:** In the film version of *The Glass Menagerie*, 1950 (Warner Bros.). **323:** Photo by Friedman-Abeles, N.Y. In *Sunrise at Campobello*. **324:** Photo by Alfredo Valente. **326:** In *The Member of the Wedding*, 1950. **327:** Photo by John Miehle for RKO Radio Pictures, 1944. **328:** Photo ca. 1969. **329:** In the film *Baby Doll*, 1956 (Warner Bros.) **330:** Columbia Pictures photo, 1967. **331:** Photo by Friedman-Abeles, N.Y.

Alphabetical Index of Performers

The numbers are those of the illustrations.